FROM
INJURY
TO ACTION:

Navigating Your Personal Injury Claim

Richard H. Adler
Attorney at Law
Adler•Giersch PS

Second Edition.
Printed in the United State of America

ISBN: 978-1-59571-771-9
Library of Congress Control Number: 2012901478

For more information about permission to reproduce selections
from this book or to order more copies, write to:

ADLER•GIERSCH ps
333 Taylor Avenue North
Seattle, WA 98109

Or email: info@adlergiersch.com

ACKNOWLEDGMENTS

A special thank you is due to so many. The idiom, "many hands make light work" takes on special meaning to me with this publication. I am grateful to the many individuals that helped in the reviews, critiques, suggestions, words of encouragement, edits, cover designs, and illustrations. The sum impact has been the shaping of an idea into something real and hopefully, useful.

My first thank you goes to my clients that I have had the honor and privilege to represent as their legal counsel and advocate. This book results from their questions about fairness with insurers, concern and worry about their physical recovery and the impact both of these worlds have had on their long-term financial recovery and emotional well-being. There is not a stronger motivation for me to write a user-friendly, information-rich guide that also exposes the dark side of the insurance process for those that experience a traumatic injury. I hope my clients will be pleased to see this work, as many have said, 'we have to tell people about what really goes on. No one has any idea about this.'

Also, I want to add a warm thank you to the many hands of health care professionals who penned comments and suggestions, particularly in Section 3 on explaining specific traumatic injuries. Thank you for taking time to emphasize how trauma can impact everything from bony structures of the body to causing inflammatory responses in cartilage, tendons, ligaments, discs, and more. The "many hands" of primary care doctors, medical specialists, surgeons, chiropractors, physical therapists, massage therapists, naturopathic physicians and acupuncturists have combined to greatly aid me in this work and as legal advocate. To the many healers, many thanks.

A special call out and acknowledgment is due to those who spent considerable time in improving the readability of this book by providing insightful and extensive valuable commentary, and working with me over time. I relied upon many of their suggestions, but take full responsibility for the contents of this book. These individuals not only served as editors, but helped move the baton from one hand to the next during the marathon run.

Lauren E. Adler. As the last name suggests, we are related. Lauren is my youngest daughter and was blessed with the gift of writing, expression, and voice from early on. Knowing good talent when I see it, I asked her during her summer break while attending Whitman College to be the first to read over the then-unfinished manuscript. As I leafed through her edits, the red mark-ups re-affirmed that she not only knew how to write and edit, but that she worked with glee at editing my writing. At the time of this second publication in 2012 Lauren will be graduating law school at Seattle University Law with a keen interest in environmental law and policy, along with legal research, writing and advocacy.

Benjamin B. Broome, M.A., Vice President of Medical Content for Medical Legal Art, the nation's leading provider of medical demon-strative evidence. Medical Legal Art is dedicated to providing a full range of solutions for the visualization of anatomy, pathology, injury and surgery as seen in Section 3 of this book. For inquiries on medical illustrations, email bbroome@medicalegalart.com.

Kristin Cruse. She is a graduate of the University of Washington and works at our law firm as the Public Relations Coordinator. Ms. Cruse also volunteers her time in the community serving on the Board of Directors of the Brain Injury Association of Washington, recently serving as its Chair of their annual Gala and Auction. I owe many thanks to the many hats she wears and the many hands she used in moving this project forward from coordinating meetings and working her magic on the drafts and re-drafts with software programs and more.

Bill Edwards. Formerly employed at a Seattle-based IT company, Bill was the person who translated the techno-speak of the programmers into an easy-to-understand presentation with illustrations and examples that sales people and the consuming public could understand. Bill is also a former client who suffered a traumatic brain injury (TBI) along with bone and musculoskeletal injuries. He saw first hand all the road-blocks, delays and tactics used by the dark side of the insurance world. Bill reviewed my manuscript with a methodical pace of no more than one section a day, a limitation imposed by his TBI and inability to process information for more than a couple of hours in a day. His insights were invaluable in transforming this into a more user-friendly resource having been there himself with a tone that tells it like it is.

Carol Fritsch. A former English language teacher, turned para-legal, she served to anchor the text with practical advise and direction. I am grateful for her efforts and teacher-style prompting to get me to rethink my approach on several passages. Ms Fritsch works at Adler Giersch.

Arthur Leritz. A special thank you to Arthur D. Leritz, my colleague and attorney at Adler Giersch PS, for agreeing to write Chapter 24, "*A Former Insurance Attorney Reveals How Insurers Defend Against Personal Injury Claims*". Mr. Leritz is no longer practicing law on behalf of insurance companies and has left the "dark side" of insurance and joined our law firm. I am grateful that Mr. Leritz shared the trade secrets of insurance attorneys. Arthur D. Leritz received his degree in Political Science from the University of Washington in 1996, followed by his Doctor of Juris-prudence from Willamette University College of Law in 1999.

Kim Runciman. She is the owner of Night Vision Edit and a free-lance editor. She tightened up everything, did a great job on copy-editing and made the text consistent throughout the book.

Janet Thoman. She received her Juris Doctorate from the University of Washington School of Law in 2006. I relied on Ms. Thoman to ensure that my legal analysis, discussion of statutes and court decision was accurate, to the point and understandable. She been a speaker for continuing legal education seminars for attorneys and healthcare provider organizations. Ms. Thoman's commitment to her clients is matched by the community service work.

Josh and Lisa Tuininga. A husband and wife dynamic duo and owners of their own graphic design firm, The Medium. They did an outstanding job of taking the content of a book and transforming it into something special with colors, images, font style and layout of content. They were the final hands that took hold of this project like the last runner of the marathon grabbing the baton and kicking hard to the finish line.

RICHARD H. ADLER
Attorney at Law, Adler Giersch PS

ABOUT THE AUTHOR

Richard H. Adler is a 1980 honors graduate of Georgetown University Law Center in Washington, D.C., where he received his Juris Doctorate degree. He was called to the Bar in Washington State that same year.

Mr. Adler is the founding principal of ADLER•GIERSCHPS, a law firm dedicated exclusively to representing victims of traumatic brain, spinal trauma, joint injuries, and musculoskeletal trauma.

Mr. Adler served as Chairman and President of the Brain Injury Association of Washington (BIA-WA) from 2003-2009, and is now serving as Chairman of the Executive Board. He is credited with turning around the BIA-WA's organization with initiatives to implement BIA-WA's mission of prevention, education, support, and advocacy for brain injury survivors and their caregivers. He led the BIA-WA's Advocacy Committee and organized a powerful coalition of healthcare, businesses, sports, and community partners to enact the "Zackery Lystedt Law," named after his client. This is the first-in-the-nation law that "prevents preventable brain injuries" of young athletes by requiring medical clearance before returning to practice or competition following a concussion.

Mr. Adler is an invited speaker and author of many publications on traumatic injuries and personal injury law for attorneys, healthcare providers, and the injured. This publication, *From Injury to Action: Navigating Your Personal Injury Claim*, joins other top-rated writings including *Understanding Traumatic Brain Injury: A Guide for Survivors and Families; Spinal Trauma and the Personal Injury Case; The Medical-Legal Aspects of Soft Tissue Injuries.* He is also published in medical journals including "Youth Sports and Concussions: Preventing Preventable Brain Injuries. One Client, One Case, and a New Law" in *Physical Medicine and Rehabilitation of North America.* (Nov 2011)

Mr. Adler and the law firm of ADLER◆GIERSCHPS are "AV" rated, the highest rating available as established in a confidential survey of other attorneys conducted by Martindale-Hubbell. He is an invited member of the Million Dollar Advocate Forum and the Multi-Million Dollar Advocate Forum, organizations of the top trial lawyers in America. He has also received the Pro Bono Award from the Washington State Bar Association every year since 2003 for his commitment and leadership in providing legal services to those in need.

In 2008, Mr. Adler received the President's Award from the American Massage Therapy Association, an award reserved for those who have advanced the profession of massage therapy statewide. In 2009, he was the first attorney ever to receive an award from the American College of Sports Medicine, the largest sports medicine and exercise science organization, for "protecting the health and safety of young athletes," for his leadership and advocacy of the Zackery Lystedt Law. Also, he has been a featured attorney profiled in the King County Bar Association's journal, *King County Bar Bulletin*, in November 2009. In 2009, he was given the Advocacy Award by the Brain Injury Association of Washington for his exemplary legal representation and advocacy for those with traumatic brain injury. In 2010, Seattle Metropolitan Magazine listed him as a "Top Lawyer" in personal injury law. Recently in 2012, Mr. Adler was awarded the Washington State Jefferson Award for his public service and was selected by other attorneys for inclusion in *Washington's Super Lawyers®*.

Mr. Adler is licensed to practice law in federal court and all jurisdictions in the State of Washington. He is a participating member of the Washington Bar Association, Washington State Association of Justice (Eagle Status), American Association for Justice, Brain Injury Association of Washington, and the Brain Injury Litigation Group.

TABLE OF CONTENTS

PART THREE – YOUR ROAD TO RECOVERY

PART FOUR – MOVING ON: YOUR SETTLEMENT

RICHARD H. ADLER
Attorney at Law, Adler Giersch PS

PART ONE

1

AFTER
YOUR PERSONAL INJURY

No *amount of money*
will replace good
health. As Aristotle
noted, "Our greatest
wealth is our health."

If you are reading this book, chances are that you have been in a motor vehicle collision or in some way injured by the fault of another person or agency. And you are not alone.

According to the National Safety Council, one in every eight drivers will be involved in a motor vehicle collision each year. If you have picked up this book, it is likely that the "one" is either you or someone you know.

Since a vast majority of traumatic injuries occur following a motor vehicle collision, this book will focus many of its pages on that area. However, I will also discuss injuries that occur when falling on someone else's property, when bitten by a dog, when using dangerous products, and other types of at-fault injury claims. And this book would not be complete without also looking into the complexities of the insurance processes, the intricacies of your injuries, ideas concerning treatment options, and how to look for and find the attorney best qualified for your case.

According to the National Safety Council, one in every eight drivers will be involved in a motor vehicle collision each year.

As you journey through these pages and your own health and financial recovery, keep in mind a few basic but critical pieces of advice:

> *The human body provides a window of opportunity for healing and rehabilitation. And that window is often early-on after a traumatic injury. Don't wait to seek help from healthcare professionals.*

✳ We all learn to appreciate our health most when we don't have it. Dedicate your time and resources to getting well because no amount of money will replace good health. As Aristotle noted, "Our greatest wealth is our health."

✳ The human body provides a window of opportunity for healing and rehabilitation. And that window is early-on after a traumatic injury. Don't wait to seek help from healthcare professionals.

✳ Do everything you can to get better, and follow your healthcare provider's recommendations. If you are not getting well with one approach, then ask your doctor for a different approach. If your doctor is not listening to you, then consider looking for another doctor or different type of healthcare provider.

✳ Educate yourself about the insurance and claims process you are going through. The insurance world can be 'stranger than fiction' at times. The more information you have, the more you can prevent insurance representatives from denying what is your legal right under contract and law.

✳ Getting the right attorney can make all the difference in the process of your case and the outcome of your case. Getting the wrong attorney can also make the difference in the process and the outcome of your case. Spend time educating yourself in what your choices are in selecting an attorney. Make sure there is a good match.

✳ Watch your back. Insurers are reaching new heights in ways to protect their profits at your expense. We now have seen the new era of training of insurance adjusters under the motto, "catch more with honey than with vinegar." Be careful and on the alert of the insurance adjuster who is friendly, sweet, or wants to be trusted by you. Remember, if they represent the other party there is no way that they can also represent you as their client or customer, regardless of their slogans and promises.

✳ Finally, ask questions. The more you know the easier it will go.

If I or any of the attorneys at the law offices of Adler Giersch, PS are able to assist you as you make your way through *From Injury to Action*, simply give us a call.

SEATTLE	206.682.0300	EVERETT	425.338.7700
BELLEVUE	425.643.0700	KENT	253.854.4500

STARTING OUT —
AT THE CRASH SCENE

CHAPTER 2

©Ocean Photography/Veer

While it may seem too late at this time, please read this section, as you may find not all of the advice is too late and should lightning strike twice you will be better prepared for the next time (and hopefully there is not a next time).

A. Safety First

When you are involved in a motor vehicle collision as the driver, passenger, bicyclist, or pedestrian:

* Stop as close and as safely as you can to the collision site and make sure the ignition of the vehicle is turned off.

* Check drivers and passengers for injuries.

* Call 911. Report the collision, location, and injuries. Wait for the police to arrive. Do not leave. Insist that the other driver(s) remain at the scene, because our experience has shown that when the at-fault driver leaves the scene before the police arrive, he/she may change their version of how the collision occurred.

* Do not move injured persons; wait until medical personnel arrive.

B. Cooperate with Police

* Remain at the scene until an officer arrives. Tell the officer how

the collision happened. Cooperate and answer all their questions to your best ability. Fully describe the events that led up to the crash and those that followed afterwards.

C. Record Information

✳ It is important to get as much information at the scene of the collision as possible. If necessary, ask a family member, friend, or witness to get this information for you if you are transported from the scene by ambulance.

✳ Write down the date, time, and location of the collision. Make note of the road and weather conditions. If the police come to the scene, record the agency (e.g. city Police, county Police, or State Patrol), the officer's name, and the *incident number*. Investigation by a police officer will often result in a written report. This report, known as the Police Traffic Collision Report, has a reference number known as the incident number.

✳ Record the names, addresses, and phone numbers of all drivers, passengers, and witnesses. Copy the other driver's information directly from his/her driver's license. Make sure to record the driver's:

☑ Name, address, and phone number

☑ Employer and work phone

☑ Make, model, and year of his/her car

☑ Name of the registered owner of the vehicle (if different than the driver)

☑ Insurance company name, agent name, and policy number(s)

☑ Driver's injuries or pain complaints, if any

☑ Any statements the driver makes to you about the collision, even if it is simply, "I'm sorry," or "I didn't see you."

✳ Write down a clear description of every vehicle involved and note anything that may have contributed to the collision. Point out these facts to the investigating police officer.

* Make a sketch of the collision scene showing the direction of travel of all vehicles, position of the vehicles at the time of impact, and the path of the vehicle from impact to stopping point. Note the location of skid marks and debris. If you or someone else has a cell phone with a camera feature, then take photos of your car, your injuries, the collision scene, and the other vehicles involved at the scene. If there is no camera available to you at the scene, then take pictures as soon as possible later on.

D. After Leaving the Collision Scene

If you have ever been involved in a collision, you know it is very difficult to remember to do everything needed, and to do it well.

However, even if you have not made notes right after the collision, try doing so now. As time goes on, specific details of the collision may become harder to remember.

RICHARD H. ADLER
Attorney at Law, Adler Giersch PS

IMPORTANT AND IMMEDIATE
CONSIDERATIONS

CHAPTER 3

A. Seek Medical Attention

If you are injured from a motor vehicle collision, it is in your best interest to seek medical attention as soon as any symptoms of achiness or pain appear.

It is common to feel fine at the scene, only to develop pain over the next several hours or days. Do not wait to seek medical attention in the hope that the pain will resolve on its own. Don't be stoic – be smart – for the sake of your health and potential claim. Are you aware that insurance claim representatives are trained to deny claims, and one of their common arguments is that the injured party did not seek healthcare immediately or shortly after the crash? They argue that *if someone is injured, then they will seek medical care; if someone does not seek medical care, then they are not injured.*

> *If you did not seek medical care early on, be prepared for your insurance company and the at-fault driver's insurer to argue that you were not hurt at all in the collision or that your injury was very minor.*

In other words, if you did not seek medical care early on, be prepared for *your* insurance company *and* the at-fault driver's insurer to argue that you were not hurt at all in the collision or that your injury was very minor.

B. Keep a Diary

Describe how the collision, pain, and physical limitations affected your work, daily routines, recreational activities, and relationships with others. Your notations can be daily, weekly, or dependent upon events that you want to make note of for future reference, e.g., activities that you used to be able to do with ease that now cause pain or limitations.

C. Consult an Attorney (for Free) Specializing in Personal Injury as Soon as Possible

Consulting with an attorney early on is a good idea. This will ensure that your rights are protected and that your insurance company or the at-fault party's insurer does not take unfair advantage of your situation. There is often no charge or fee for an initial consultation. Whether you will need to actually hire a lawyer can best be decided after a consultation. And if the attorney is needed in your case, then having an attorney on board earlier accomplishes more in the long run, and costs you nothing extra. *And remember, do not sign any papers or cash any checks from any insurance company (even your own insurer) until you have consulted an attorney.*

D. Do I Have to Give Tape-Recorded Statements to the Insurance Companies?

After reporting the collision to *your* insurance company, you must cooperate with their investigation of your claim. However, this does not necessarily mean that you must go along with everything, particularly if it undermines your claim *and* is not specifically required in your insurance policy. For example, your insurer will want to take a tape-recorded statement with you over the phone or in person. They will insist that you have "a duty to cooperate" with your own insurance company. However, although you do have a duty to cooperate with your own insurer, it does not require giving a tape-recorded statement, unless this is specifically detailed in your insurance policy. *Tape-recorded statements can and will be used against you, not only for what you say, but for what you do not say.* If your insurer refuses to act on your claim until you provide a tape-recorded statement, insist they show you the provision in your insurance policy that requires one. Chances are, they will not be able to. *Just say no.*

While you do have a duty to cooperate with your own insurance company under the terms of your insurance policy, there is no duty to cooperate with the at-fault party's insurer. Never, ever provide the at-fault party's insurer with a tape-recorded statement. For example,

Jane gave a taped-recorded statement to the at-fault party's insurer:

> Q: Have you ever had neck pain before?
>
> A: No. This is the first time, and it is not fun.
>
> Q: You never, ever had neck pain before?
>
> A: That is correct.

However, Jane had been to a chiropractor before for her lower back. Unknown to Jane was a notation by her chiropractor that he adjusted her neck when working on correcting her lower back. The insurer then took the taped-statement and used it in a way to attack Jane's credibility.

Refusing to give a taped or digitally recorded statement with an insurance company has nothing to do with hiding information. It has to do with an insurer's motivation to trap you and use information against you at a later time.

E. Should I Settle My Injury Claim Early On, Since the Adjuster Seems So Friendly and Eager?

It seems logical that if a person with a traumatic injury presents a reasonable claim, then his or her insurance company will act reasonably as well. Unfortunately, insurance companies do not live by this rule. Despite TV and radio ads, insurance is not your neighbor, friend, or a caretaker who always holds you in "good hands."

The at-fault driver's insurer is concerned with protecting their insured and the insurance company's profits. This means that an insurance company will often try to settle claims early – for them, settling early means cheaply, regardless of your short or long-term healthcare needs.

A check for a few thousand dollars on the spot days after a traumatic injury "if you only sign here" may sound very tempting . . . but injuries often take days, weeks, and even many months to fully express themselves.

The insurers train and coach their claims representatives (also known as adjusters) to try to get an injured party to sign a release of all claims early on by using "honey, not vinegar" approaches. While it might be tempting to accept settlement money at such a stressful time, here are some important points to keep in mind:

* It is not uncommon for symptoms to be delayed in their onset after the initial trauma. Sometimes it can take weeks or months for symptoms to appear. Also, sometimes symptoms that seem mild initially will worsen and cause moderate or severe pain and/or limitations in daily activities.

* An injury can cause post-traumatic arthritis which rarely shows up on X-rays until at least 6 months and often much later than that.

* Until a doctor believes that recovery is complete and states that you have reached pre-injury condition, you cannot be reasonably certain that there will not be late-developing symptoms or future medical expenses.

> *It seems logical that if a person with a traumatic injury presents a reasonable claim, then his or her insurance company will act reasonably as well. Unfortunately, insurance companies do not live by this rule.*

* Once the insurance company's release is signed, the matter is final. Should problems develop later, there is no recourse and it is nearly impossible to reopen your claim. All post-settlement expenses related to the collision will be your responsibility.

* If your injury was caused by another person's negligence, you are entitled to compensation for pain and suffering, medical expenses, wage loss, and other financial losses. It is not in the insurance company's financial interests to fully disclose their legal obligations and your legal rights regarding compensation owed to you.

PART TWO

2

HARD FACTS
ABOUT INSURANCE

YOUR RIGHTS WITH YOUR
INSURANCE COMPANY

CHAPTER 4

If you are the driver or passenger and have been injured in a motor vehicle collision in Washington, you likely have Personal Injury Protection (PIP) coverage.

This means that if you have been injured in a motor vehicle collision, the insurance company for the car you occupy (as driver or passenger) will be involved in paying medical expenses as they are initially incurred up to the amount of coverage purchased by the owner of the PIP insurance policy, typically $10,000 per person in your car, but it may be as high as $25,000 or $35,000 per person.

As an insured person, you surely expect your insurance company to be in your corner during a time of need. After all, you purchase insurance for peace of mind, in case something bad happens. However, many insurance carriers use "cost-containment" strategies in order to pay as little as possible on claims like yours, or go so far as to deny your treatment bills entirely.

> *As an insured person, you surely expect your insurance company to be in your corner during a time of need. After all, you purchase insurance for peace of mind, in case something bad happens.*

For example, your own auto insurance company may hire its own doctors to review your healthcare records or require you to be evaluated by the doctor of their choosing. A PIP insurer may refer to this as an *Independent Medical Examination* or IME. Don't be misled by the word "independent." It is not independent at all. Experienced attorneys in personal injury and insurance law have nicknamed the IME as the *Involuntary Medical Examination* or an *Insurance Medical*

Examination, as these exams are most often conducted by "hired guns" from the insurer. An IME is designed as a cost-containment strategy to undermine your need for treatment by cutting off medical bills. This results in more money in the insurer's pocket. For example, the IME examiner can conclude that you require no additional treatment or that the condition is not related to the collision. Why would an IME doctor do such a thing? Because they make a lot of money at it. Many of the doctors used by insurers to conduct such examinations either do this work exclusively, or receive a large part of their livelihood from this type of work. It is important to seek a legal consultation with an attorney experienced in personal injury law *before* an IME to make sure your rights to treatment and payment of bills are protected. An experienced attorney has many options to neutralize or level the playing field. However, it is best to consult with the attorney before the IME, not afterwards.

> *An IME is designed as a cost-containment strategy to undermine your need for treatment by cutting off medical bills. This results in more money in the insurer's pocket.*

DO I NEED AN ATTORNEY?

Traumatic injury claims *can* be settled without attorney representation. However, laws related to traumatic injuries are complex and change frequently.

Insurance companies are well aware of the written and unwritten rules, but most injury victims are not. The insurance company will not explain these rules to you; keeping you in the dark will only help them.

An attorney, however, represents *your* interests, not those of the other driver or the insurance companies. Good legal counsel will research and analyze the facts regarding your claim, work with your healthcare providers, prepare documents, and negotiate a fair and reasonable settlement.

In personal injury cases, most attorneys are paid on a contingency fee basis. This means that the attorney's fee, usually one-third of the final settlement, is not paid until the case is concluded.

In Washington, the Statute of Limitations (see Chapter 29, pages 110–113 for more information on this) for a motor vehicle collision claim is three years. This means that your case must be either concluded with a mutually agreeable settlement within three years of the date of the collision, or you must make sure that a lawsuit is filed in court before that time in order to preserve your legal rights. (For minors, the three-year Statute of

Limitations to file a lawsuit only starts once the child reaches his/her eighteenth birthday). If the collision occurred in another state, the Statute of Limitations timeline may be different than in Washington, as each state is free to set its own Statute of Limitations laws and timetables. It is best to consult an attorney early in the process to determine the time limit in your case.

> *Insurance companies are well aware of the written and unwritten rules, but most injury victims are not. The insurance company will not explain these rules to you; keeping you in the dark will only help them.*

Whether you hire an attorney or not is likely one of the most important decisions following a trauma. I recommend reading Chapter 29 of this book at pages 110–113 to review the questions of: do I need an attorney?; how long will it take to settle?; what will an attorney do for me or my family?; what should I expect when hiring an attorney?; and other practical information.

YOUR HEALTH AND ECONOMIC RECOVERY V. THE INSURER'S PROFITS

CHAPTER 6

Dealing with insurance forms, body shops, insurance claim representatives, and a flood of new information can be overwhelming. Add to this the fact that you or a loved one is recovering from injuries and it can become all-consuming.

After the initial flurry of activity simmers down, an injured person may wonder how they should approach decisions and how these decisions will affect the ultimate resolution of their claim.

> *The most important consideration for you as an injured person is your physical and emotional well-being. Therefore, decisions should be guided by what is best for your health and recovery.*

Your Needs v. Profits

The most important consideration for you as an injured person is your physical and emotional well-being. Therefore, decisions should be guided by what is best for *your* health and recovery. The insurance company's goal has nothing to do with ensuring that you recover 100 percent or that you get proper healthcare, despite marketing slogans such as "you're in good hands" and "like a good neighbor."

Remember, insurance is a for-profit business. They make greater profits when they pay out the least amount possible, regardless of your losses and needs.

Insurers that pay medical expenses or other benefits as they are incurred, such as Personal Injury Protection or MedPay carriers, want to keep expenditures to a minimum. At-fault insurers are also interested in paying out the least amount possible. *You* must look out for *your* interests and *your* healthcare needs. Do not count on your insurance company or the at-fault party's insurance company to do this for you.

In order to take care of your health and physical concerns, you as the injured party must address a variety of issues. Your own insurance company, under your Personal Injury Protection policy, can create obstacles that interfere with your access to healthcare and your ability to recover from the injuries. They may delay payment of bills or require that you get evaluated by one of their "independent" doctors (see Chapter 21 in this book).

The financial impact of traumatic injuries can be mild to severe. Physical *and* emotional recovery is important for the injured party, but so is your financial recovery. There are "legal" or "evidence-based" requirements in the claim process to obtain financial compensation for losses incurred. The fundamental rule of managing the financial side of your claim is *document everything*. Keep detailed receipts of all expenses. If income loss is an issue, ask your doctor to write down your restrictions and have your employer provide written confirmation of what benefits were lost, such as pay, vacation time, or sick days. If you send a letter or email to an insurance adjuster or healthcare provider, always keep a hardcopy for your file. Also, keep a diary of your own thoughts and experiences as details will be difficult to recall later. This will also aid your attorney, if one is needed, in establishing and effectively presenting your personal injury claim.

If it appears that your insurance company or the other party's insurer is placing their business interests ahead of your own (which is not unusual), then it is time to seek legal consultation with an attorney specializing in personal injury law. Locate such an attorney by talking to people you trust and respect. Generally, a word-of-mouth referral will provide the name of someone who has been tested, achieved a good result, and has pleased former clients. Be cautious of attorneys that advertise on television or in the yellow pages. See pages 124–126, "Lawyer Advertising and What You Need to Know," for some of the hidden facts about law firm advertisement.

INSURANCE — INTRODUCTION

Depending on the circumstances of the motor vehicle collision or nature of injury, there may be several different types of insurance coverages that relate to your physical, economic, and emotional recovery.

Each coverage provides a certain type of benefit. Some pay only medical bills, while others cover those bills and any additional income loss. Some policies protect you, the insured party, such as Personal Injury Protection or PIP. Other policies protect the at-fault party, such as liability coverage. It is important to identify and coordinate the various policies in order to ensure that you reach physical and financial recovery.

I recommend that you as the injured party learn which policies are available, the scope of each policy and the respective rights and responsibilities under each. You may be surprised by what you learn.

Failure to properly understand and coordinate the available coverages may significantly reduce your financial recovery. It can result in the loss of your rights, impede access to healthcare, and result in significant other financial losses.

In the next several pages we will discuss various insurance policies that may be available to you and how they aid your physical, emotional, and financial recovery.

INSURANCE —
AUTO PROPERTY DAMAGE
CHAPTER 8

If your collision was another's driver's fault, that person's insurance company will be responsible for compensating you for your losses. The property damage to your car should be handled by the at-fault

©iStockphoto.com/Frances Twitty

party's insurance coverage. However, it is not uncommon for this insurer to take more time than you can wait for the claim process to get started. This can be very frustrating, as your car is likely needed for work, shopping, or transporting family members.

If you purchased collision coverage from your own insurer, you can often get your vehicle repaired more quickly. Your auto insurer will then get reimbursed from the at-fault insurer later on.

Property damage claims can be resolved in one of two ways: either your car can be repaired or it can be declared a total loss – meaning that the cost of the repair exceeds the value of the car.

It's worth remembering that damage to your car based on a *visual inspection only* may leave hidden frame damage unrepaired. When frame damage is properly inspected and assessed it could result in significant extra costs for repairs.

RICHARD H. ADLER
Attorney at Law, Adler Giersch PS

DEALING WITH INSURANCE COMPANIES

When handling your property damage claim, here are a few tips to keep in mind.

A. Choice of Automotive Repair Shop

When your car has been damaged, you have the right to have it repaired at a shop of your choice. There is no obligation to use a shop chosen by the insurance company.

B. Property Damage "Release"

Do not sign any type of "Release of Claims" for property damage until the vehicle has been returned to you in pre-collision condition. Take your car for a test drive and look it over carefully. Make sure you are satisfied that your car has been returned to its pre-collision condition before signing any insurance company check or property damage release; otherwise, you may waive your right to further repairs.

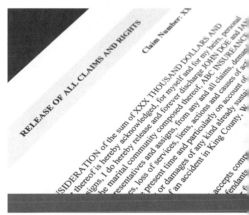

C. Car Repairs

You have the right to have your car repaired at the body shop of your choice. You do not have to use the insurer's "recommended" or "preferred" body shop. Also, you need not accept the insurance company's property damage appraisal of the actual repair costs. You may take your car to your own body shop and then present a written estimate to the insurance company.

D. Total Loss

When your car is labeled a *total loss*, the insurance company must make payment of the *market value* of your car for the condition it was in immediately before the collision. Market value can be determined by looking through classified ads, asking a car dealer what a comparable car sells for on their lots, or searching online for a similar car with similar mileage.

In negotiating the value of your car, let the insurance company know of recent repairs, special accessories, and the value of any damaged contents. The *market value* of your car is generally higher than the *blue book value*.

> *The market value of your car is generally higher than the blue book value.*

A word of caution if you have a leased car or are making monthly payments to the bank: your auto insurer (under the collision coverage of your policy) and the at-fault party's insurance (under the liability part of that person's policy) are not responsible for an outstanding loan or lease balance that may exceed the vehicle's market value. Cars that depreciate quickly once driven off the car dealer's lot may result in payments greater than the car's actual worth. If you are making monthly payments, you may end up owing more than the car is actually worth. This is called being upside down in a loan/lease arrangement with the lender, and you are responsible for the balance. For example, if you have a $15,000 balance on your loan and the car is totaled with a market value of $12,000 then you will have to pay the $3,000 out of your pocket.

E. Rental Car

If the collision was someone else's fault, that person's insurance company must provide you with a rental car while your car is not functional. You have the right to either a rental car or daily compensation for the loss of use of your property (car). If there is a delay in obtaining a rental car, you are entitled to compensation for the loss of your vehicle for each day you are deprived of its use; this is another part of a property damage claim.

If your car is deemed a total loss, rental coverage extends from the date of the collision to when the responsible insurance company declared the car totaled.

If the at-fault driver is *uninsured*, your right to a rental car is subject to the terms of your own insurance policy.

When a car is rented, you will not need additional rental car property damage insurance *if* you have collision coverage on your vehicle. If you *do not have* collision coverage, you will be required to pay for coverage on the rental car by the rental car company.

Note: most car rental companies want business and usually have drop-off and pick-up services at no additional charge.

F. Diminished Value

When your vehicle is damaged by the fault of another, then his/her insurer is responsible for the full cost of repairs so that your vehicle is restored to its pre-loss condition. But once a car is in a collision and then repaired, it has lost some of its value. Have you ever tried to sell your car back to the dealership following a collision, even when repairs have been made? The dealer will say that the car is no longer worth its pre-crash value even with a full repair. There remains property damage that cannot be repaired, e.g., weakened metal that won't withstand another crash, or perhaps the crash now impacts the car's longevity.

As part of your property damage claim, it is reasonable to request that your car get repaired and that you be compensated for your property's post-repair "diminished value." One way to obtain the information on your car's diminished value is to ask folks at your dealership.

G. General Guidelines

1. *Take pictures.* Take photographs of the vehicle damage at the scene of the collision or soon afterward and have them printed or stored on a CD.

2. *Sign a property damage release only.* Be sure that any check you endorse clearly states that it is a settlement for property damage only – not a release for *all* claims, and not a release of bodily injury or personal injury claims. Sign this only after you have inspected the repairs to your car and taken it for a test drive. Sign no other releases.

3. *Do not discuss any matters concerning your injuries with the at-fault insurance company.* You are under no obligation to give any information concerning your injuries and treatment. Discuss

nothing but property damage and the need for a rental car or "loss of use" compensation, even if the insurance adjuster seems friendly and asks "How are you?" Simply say that you will follow up with them on injuries and treatment later on.

4. *Beware of the clever insurance adjuster.* Avoid taking your car to the insurance company shop or drive-through service. It provides the adjuster with an opportunity to take photographs of you, observe you getting in and out of the car, bending down to pick up keys, etc. Insurance claims representatives can be very coy. While dealing with your property damage, they may take the opportunity to evaluate your injuries, your lifestyle, or you as a person. This information could later be used against you if you decide to make a claim for bodily injury. Ask a friend to take your car in for the damage appraisal, or request that the insurance company representative go to the location of your parked car rather than you traveling to them.

> *Avoid taking your car to the insurance company shop or drive-through service.*

INSURANCE — PERSONAL INJURY PROTECTION (PIP)

In many types of motor vehicle collisions, the injured party often will have insurance to cover *some* of the out-of-pocket losses under the terms of their own automobile insurance policy as the expenses are incurred.

However, the at-fault party's liability insurer has *no* obligation to pay the injured party's medical or economic losses as they arise (except the property damage claims as they must be handled within approximately 30 days of the collision under Washington law), and they will generally make only one payment when a claim is finally settled, even if it's months or years later.

Many car insurance policies in Washington include a provision known as *Personal Injury Protection* or *PIP* for short. This coverage pays for collision-related medical expenses up to a set limit, regardless of fault. Under this coverage, there are no co-pays or deductibles, and collision-related medical bills are paid at 100 percent. In Washington, the minimum PIP limit is $10,000 (though higher limits are available for purchase). This means that the PIP insurer will pay up to $10,000 in collision-related medical expenses for up to three years. This coverage applies to each person in the insured vehicle. For example, if you are driving with two passengers, you and each passenger have a separate $10,000 limit for individual healthcare bills.

PIP also covers a certain portion of collision-related income loss. If a driver cannot work as a result of injuries incurred in the collision, the PIP policy will pay *a portion* of the lost wages. Most policies exclude the first two weeks after the collision, so there is no coverage for wages lost during those first 14 days after the injury. Additionally, PIP will cover only 85 percent of your regular income, up to a limit of $200 per week. This means that if you were not able to work for a full year, then your PIP wage benefit is $200 per week, or $10,000 for the entire year. On policies with higher PIP medical limits, such as $35,000, the wage loss coverage limit will be $700 per week.

> *Personal Injury Protection, or PIP for short, pays for collision-related medical expenses up to a set limit, regardless of fault.*

A third benefit offered in your PIP policy in Washington is an allowance for household services help. If, due to your injury, you are unable to perform household chores such as cleaning or yard work, PIP coverage also provides a daily stipend to hire someone to perform these services. This amount is usually $40 a day, unless you have a higher level of PIP coverage.

To obtain medical benefits under a PIP policy, your doctor's records must show that your treatment and any referrals to other healthcare providers meet the "reasonable, necessary, and related to the collision" standard. This language is contained in your PIP policy and is the standard that governs payment of your medical expenses.

To obtain wage-loss benefits under a PIP policy, your doctor must provide a written work restriction, complete with a start and end date. The PIP insurer will also require confirmation of employment and wage information before they will provide PIP wage loss compensation.

To obtain *loss of services* benefits under a PIP policy, your doctor must state, in writing, that you are unable to perform household chores and that you require assistance. Again, the doctor's statement must include a start and end date, and be updated as needed. Your PIP insurer will compensate you for household services only *after* the expenses are paid by you. Itemized receipts must be submitted showing, at a minimum, the name of the person performing the work, dates worked, services performed, and payment per day. If using the PIP household services benefit, you are not allowed to average the $40 per day benefit. For example, if your loss of services benefit is $40 per day, the expense must be incurred *each day* for $40. Hired household help could not work one full day per week and charge $200 for that day (5 days x $40 per day). Regardless of the amount of work performed on a single day, the maximum payment reimbursable under PIP coverage would be $40 per day.

PIP coverage limits and requirements vary. If PIP is available, it is important to obtain a copy of the PIP policy to determine what coverage is available and for how long.

> *To obtain medical benefits under a PIP policy, your doctor's records must show that your treatment and any referrals to other healthcare providers meet the "reasonable, necessary, and related to the collision" standard. This language is contained in your PIP policy and is the standard that governs payment of your medical expenses.*

Many people are reluctant to access their own PIP coverage for fear it will negatively affect their insurance rate or renewability. However, if you are not at-fault, then your insurer cannot use this incident to increase your rates, non-renew your policy, or cancel coverage. The law in Washington is clear that no policy of insurance can be canceled, nonrenewed, denied, or have the rate increased unless the policyholder was determined to be at fault in the accident. The Revised Code of Washington (RCW) states, in part:

> Any insurance company or its agent receiving the certified abstract shall use it exclusively for its own underwriting purposes and shall not divulge any of the information contained in it to a third party. No policy of insurance may be canceled, nonrenewed, denied or have the rate increased on the basis of such information unless the policyholder was determined to be at fault. . . . [1]

Moreover, it is not effective to try to get your health insurance to leap frog ahead of PIP coverage and cover medical care from an auto collision. All healthcare insurance policies in Washington contain a

---

1   Quoting from RCW 46.52.130 (Title 46, Chapter 52, Section 130)

provision that requires an insured involved in a collision to first exhaust any PIP benefits before the health insurer will cover any accident-related bills. This is called Coordination of Benefits.

A. PIP Dispute: Arbitration Resolution Process

When an injured party has a conflict with his or her insurance company, it often involves the insurer's refusal to pay medical expenses under the PIP policy based upon an Independent (Involuntary or Insurer-mandated as we call it) "Medical Examination" (IME). Remember — never submit to this examination without talking to your attorney. Read more about how insurers use IMEs to deny your treatment bills in Chapters 21-23.

The option of resolving a dispute about payment of an outstanding bill is available only to the insured and his/her attorney, and not to your doctor or therapist. Your healthcare providers may be indirect beneficiaries of the PIP policy, but they have no legal right to challenge an insurer's refusal to pay its bill. The action must come from you, the insured, because it is you that has the contract with your insurer. You paid premiums to your insurance company in exchange for a promise to cover medical expenses in the event of a motor vehicle collision. If your insurer does not cover the bills, then you are the only one who can claim that the insurer breached the terms of the insurance policy or, essentially, broke its promise to you.

Most PIP policies in Washington state provide for resolution of disputes through an arbitration process. When a dispute arises in a PIP claim, most insurance policies have a provision similar to the following:

> If we and a person seeking PIP coverage do not agree on
> the amount payable under this coverage, the matter shall,
> upon mutual written agreement, be decided by arbitration.

PIP arbitration is a forum for resolving disputes that is intended to be less costly and time consuming than filing a lawsuit. Arbitrators are attorneys who have experience in hearing cases and making a decision. In arbitration, each side presents its evidence to the arbitrator(s), who then determines the result. Most arbitration decisions are binding, which means that both parties must abide by the arbitrator's decision and the matter is then considered closed. No appeal is possible.

Your PIP policy will probably specify whether the arbitration is heard by a single arbitrator or by a panel of three arbitrators. If the parties agree on a specific arbitrator, that person will hear and decide the matter. If the parties cannot agree, each party will choose an arbitrator and, together, choose a third. A decision is made based on the agreement of two out of the three arbitrators.

Choosing an arbitrator is a very important part of the PIP dispute resolution process. Arbitrators have differing professional backgrounds and experiences. There are many arbitration service businesses that can provide a list of available arbitrators from which to choose. If you have hired an attorney, he/she will select an arbitrator that has the experience to understand the issues presented and the rights and duties of all involved.

B. Insurance Dispute With Your Automobile Insurer: Filing a Claim Under the Insurance Fair Conduct Act (IFCA)

The Insurance Fair Conduct Act (IFCA) is relatively recent. It was made effective December 6, 2007.

It provides legal remedies for policy holders. If you establish that your claim was unreasonably or even illegally denied by your insurance company, there are specific monetary remedies available such as paying the medical bills that have been held hostage, attorney fees and costs in litigating the issue, and punitive damages of up to three times the amount of the IFCA claim.

> *If you establish that your claim was unreasonably or even illegally denied by your insurance company, there are specific monetary remedies available such as paying the medical bills that have been held hostage, attorney fees and costs.*

Prior to IFCA, there were laws and regulations that required insurance companies to acknowledge their policy holders' letters and phone calls about their claims, promptly investigate claims, and fairly settle valid claims. But there was no meaningful remedy for the policy holder when the insurer violated the rules. This made for an unfair advantage, as the cost to challenge your insurance company's decision was expensive and the outcome, even when you won, was just to get the disputed bills paid. Now, under IFCA, when your insurance company violates these rules and standards, you can seek meaningful remedies that require the insurer to pay more attention to the needs of its insured (you).

The law applies only to claims made by you against your own insurance company, not against someone else's insurance company. For example, if you have been in a motor vehicle collision, IFCA does *not* apply to your claim against the at-fault person's policy. Another limitation of the law is that it does not apply to claims you might make against your health insurance policy, e.g., Regence, Premera, Aetna, etc.

IFCA requires policy holders intending to sue their insurance company to mail written notice of the potential lawsuit to both the insurance company and to the Office of the Insurance Commissioner at least 20 days before the lawsuit is to be filed. Chances are, if you are going to pursue an IFCA claim against your auto insurer, you'll want to have an attorney on your side to navigate the waters.

Insurance — MedPay for Injuries on Property

CHAPTER 10

When a traumatic injury occurs on another person's or business' property, there is usually a PIP-like type of coverage specifically for this type of situation. It is known as MedPay (short for medical payments). MedPay and PIP policies are designed to give the injured party a small pool of money to cover immediate emergency medical bills without a determination of who is at-fault.

This coverage will pay medical expenses for anyone injured on the owner's property up to a set limit, often $1,000 to $5,000 which is not very much. Similar to PIP insurance, this coverage does not require payment of deductibles and co-payments. However, the medical expenses must be directly related to an injury that occurred on some person's or business' property. MedPay policies generally do not cover any expenses other than a limited amount of medical bills.

Insurance — Health Insurance

CHAPTER 11

Your health insurance plan may also provide benefits for trauma-related treatment needs when:

1. There is no PIP or MedPay available; or
2. PIP or MedPay benefits have been exhausted.

However, health insurance policies work differently than the auto insurance PIP coverage. For example, PIP covers 100 percent of the healthcare bill with no co-pays or deductible owed by the insured. When health insurance steps in after PIP coverage is exhausted, the treatment bills will now be subject to your own health insurance policy, which may include deductibles and co-pays.

Many people injured in a car collision often do not want to contact their auto insurer to obtain PIP benefits and will try to have all treatment bills sent to their health insurance plan. This approach does *not* work and will result in delayed payment of bills, with more stress and headaches for you. Why? The answer is contained in the Coordination of Benefits provision of every health insurance policy. This provision requires that injury-related treatment bills be submitted through PIP or MedPay policies *before* the health insurer will pay.

In other words, in a motor vehicle collision, PIP is the primary insurer and the health insurance is the secondary insurer. The health insurance policy only gets activated after the primary insurance (PIP) is exhausted (or if it does not exist).

There may also be other provisions within a health insurance policy that must be followed in order to have the bills covered. For example, does your policy require your primary care physician (PCP) to make the referral to see a specialist? Does your policy put a cap or limitation on the number of treatments you can have in a year with a chiropractor, physical therapist, acupuncturist, or licensed massage therapist? It's a good idea to know about these provisions in your policy, as there is a great deal of variability from one insurer to the next and even within policies issued by the same insurer. Ultimately, when your case is settled you may be able to recover any out of pocket expenses such as deductibles, co-pays, and treatment services not covered by your health insurance.

In a motor vehicle collision, PIP is the primary insurer and the health insurance is the secondary insurer. The health insurance policy only gets activated after the primary insurance (PIP) is exhausted (or if it does not exist).

If your healthcare provider is a "preferred" or "participating" provider with your health insurance plan, there will often be a requirement that they bill the health insurer for your treatment. However, the healthcare provider will be paid a reduced amount when compared to what is billed. In this situation the provider cannot hold their bill until the end of the case intending to get full payment at that time. However, if the provider does not have a contract with your insurer, they may hold your bill and collect the outstanding balance when you settle your claim.

INSURANCE — SUBROGATION

CHAPTER 12

Once your automobile insurer provides PIP benefits, or if your health insurer pays treatment bills for your injuries, then anticipate each insurer claiming the right to be reimbursed . . . *if* (and only if) you receive a settlement or verdict in your traumatic injury case.

> *Subrogation provisions can have an enormous impact on the bottom-line outcome of a case.*

This is called "subrogation" and will be contained in the insurance policy. It may also be referred to as the health insurer's "right of reimbursement."

The insurer's claim for subrogation or reimbursement may not be valid under Washington law. The wording of the insurer's actual contract language is important to review and understand. There are many instances in which the insurer's right to be reimbursed from the settlement with the at-fault insurer will be void or limited under Washington law. Having a consultation with an experienced personal injury attorney on this issue would be wise and valuable in making informed decisions that best protect your rights and interests.

Subrogation provisions can have an enormous impact on the bottom-line outcome of a case. For example, let's say your injuries resulted in $25,000 of medical bills. Of this amount, $10,000 was paid by your PIP coverage and the other $15,000 by your health insurer. Then the at-fault party agrees to settle your claim for $25,000. You may think you get to keep the $25,000. However, after the final settlement release is signed, you may get a letter or phone call from the PIP insurer claiming its right to be reimbursed for the $10,000 in medical benefits paid from your $25,000 settlement. Next, you receive a letter from the health insurer claiming a right to the $15,000 in bills they paid. All of a sudden, the person who thought they had achieved a $25,000 settlement will be faced with a lot of stress and anxiety, and ultimately receive nothing.

However, this situation has a dramatically different outcome with an experienced personal injury attorney. If the $25,000 settlement was the maximum liability insurance that was purchased by the at-fault party, then the proper legal argument by your attorney is that the PIP and healthcare insurers are not entitled to *any* reimbursement since you were not fully compensated for all your injuries, losses, and pain and/or suffering under Washington law. The subrogation rights of your PIP or healthcare insurer are only triggered after you have been fully compensated. And if there was only $25,000 available for insurance coverage and $25,000 was obtained from the at-fault party's insurer, it means that the injured party can claim that he was not fully compensated and that he was limited by the insufficient amount of the liability insurance available. As a result, the injured party collects the full $25,000 (less attorney fees) and does not have to repay the subrogation claims. This is a substantially better result than having to forfeit all $25,000 of the settlement, to the PIP insurer ($10,000) and to his health insurer ($15,000).

The law of subrogation is complex, ever-changing, and confusing. For example, the rights of the injured person to be fully compensated before the PIP insurer or health insurer can claim a subrogation right to be reimbursed for payment of bills may be different if the insurer's policy is based on federal laws instead of Washington State laws.

An attorney can negotiate a significant reduction in the subrogation or reimbursement claims of the PIP or health insurers in ways that an unrepresented individual cannot, resulting in a better financial recovery for the injured party.

Also, even in situations where the final settlement amount represents a full settlement that is less than the full policy limits, an attorney can negotiate a significant reduction in the subrogation or reimbursement claims of the PIP or health insurers in ways that an unrepresented individual cannot, resulting in a better financial recovery for the injured party.

RICHARD H. ADLER
Attorney at Law, Adler Giersch PS

Insurance — Liability

Liability insurance coverage is an essential element of any insurance policy – it acts as a shield to protect the at-fault party's assets if he/she causes an injury to you.

Liability coverage is mandatory on all automobiles in Washington. The "mandatory minimum" amount of liability coverage is the "25/50/10" policy. This means that for each collision caused by the at-fault policy-holder, the insurer will cover the losses of the non-at-fault injured party up to, but not more than, $25,000 per person; and up to, but not more than, $50,000 for all injuries to two or more victims; and up to, but not more than, $10,000 for property damage in a collision. If you are at-fault in a motor vehicle collision, your liability coverage is responsible for all the medical treatment, economic losses, inconveniences, and property damage caused to the non-at-fault party.

© Radius Images/Inmagine

If your injuries are caused by the fault of the other driver, then that driver's liability insurance pays for your property damage and personal injury claims . . . but only up to the amount of coverage purchased by the other driver.

If your injuries exceed the amount of liability coverage of the at-fault party, you can tap into another layer of insurance coverage called *Underinsured Coverage*. We will cover this in the next chapter.

Typical limits for liability coverage offered include 25/50/10, 50/100/25, 100/300/50, and 250/500/250. A driver with a 25/50/10 policy who causes moderate or significant bodily harm to just one person will have only $25,000 to pay for the losses, injuries, and damages even though they may be higher than that amount of coverage. A driver with only a 25/50/10 liability policy that causes a four-car pile up will likely have insufficient coverage for the property damage or bodily injury claims of the four different cars. Once the liability policy limit of the at-fault driver's policy has been exhausted, their personal assets (home, auto, bank account, retirement account, or other assets) may become subject to legal action by the injured victim(s) to pay the remaining amounts owed.

Before I jump into explaining uninsured/underinsured coverage, it is important to point out that under Washington law, the at-fault party's liability insurer has no obligation to pay any medical bills, loss of income, disability, or pain and suffering damages as the bills or losses are incurred. The liability insurer will only pay for medical bills, wage loss, out-of-pocket expenses, and pain and suffering damages when the injured party is prepared to settle the entire claim. This is well-established law in Washington, but can differ from state to state. As a result, if you are injured in a motor vehicle collision, your treatment bills should be paid by the PIP insurer (don't wait for the liability insurer to help out at this point because they are not required to do so). When the PIP coverage is exhausted, the bills can get redirected to your health insurer for payment as you get the treatment you need. Don't avoid using your PIP or health insurance coverage thinking that the at-fault insurer will step up and pay right away. They are not required to and they won't.

RICHARD H. ADLER
Attorney at Law, Adler Giersch PS

INSURANCE — UNINSURED AND UNDERINSURED MOTORIST

CHAPTER 14

Statutory laws (the ones approved by the state legislature) for the state of Washington mandate that insurers selling auto insurance policies must offer Uninsured Motorist insurance (UM) and Underinsured Motorist insurance (UIM) to those persons purchasing liability automobile insurance, in the same amount as the liability insurance purchased.

The Washington Supreme Court in 1985 interpreted the legislative purpose behind the UM/UIM statute as ensuring the availability of a source of recovery to the innocent victim of an auto collision when the at-fault party does not provide adequate protection.[1]

Simply defined, Uninsured and Underinsured Motorists coverage provides you compensation benefits if you are injured by another driver who has no or minimum liability insurance coverage. Liability insurance is required by law but many drivers do not have coverage. Typically, UM and UIM are contained in the same section of an automobile insurance policy and the premium paid is for both UM and UIM coverages.

> *Simply defined, Uninsured and Underinsured Motorists coverage provides you compensation benefits if you are injured by another driver who has no or minimum liability insurance coverage.*

---

1   See *Britton v. Safeco*, 104 Wn.2nd 518, 531, 707, P2d 125 (1985) and *Elovich v. Nationwide Ins. Co.*, 104 Wn.2d 543, 707 P.2d 1319 (1985).

The statutory scheme surrounding UM and UIM coverage mandates all auto insurers to offer UM/UIM coverage to Washington policy holders. Also, the law requires auto insurers to offer UM/UIM coverage in the same amount as the liability insurance purchased.

For example, if you have purchased liability insurance of $100,000 to protect your assets in case you are at-fault, then the law requires the auto insurer to offer you UM/UIM coverage of $100,000 to protect you against the at-fault driver who has no insurance (uninsured) or insufficient insurance (underinsured).

Waivers

Though UM/UIM coverage must be "offered" to an insured, you can *waive* (not purchase it) the coverage entirely or purchase an amount less than the liability coverage. This means your insurance company is required to offer this coverage to you, but you have no legal duty to accept it. However, it is a very unwise decision to not carry UM/UIM coverage. Did you know that a significant number of injury-related crashes are caused by drivers who have no insurance or very little insurance?

If the written waiver has not been signed by the insured **or** *the insurance company cannot produce a copy of the waiver it claims was signed by the insured, then your insurance company is required to retroactively provide UM/UIM coverage in the same amount as the liability coverage.*

If you do not accept the UM/UIM coverage, Washington law requires that the insured *shall* sign a written waiver of coverage.[2] Interestingly (and something not widely known by consumers, healthcare providers, and even many attorneys), if the written waiver has not been signed by the insured *or* the insurance company cannot produce a copy of the waiver it claims was signed by the insured, then your insurance company is required to retroactively provide UM/UIM coverage in the same amount as the liability coverage at the time of the motor vehicle accident. In a 1993 Washington Supreme Court decision in the case of *Clements v. Travelers Indemnity Company*,[3] the court set out a number of important legal principles:

2   RCW (Revised Code of Washington) 48.22.030 (4)
3   121 Wn.2d 243, 850 P.2d 1298 (1993)

1. UIM coverage is mandatory unless the insured makes a valid written rejection.

2. The UM/UIM statute reflects the legislative intent "to place upon the insurer [company] the burden of obtaining a knowing written rejection in order to avoid the statutory requirement for UIM coverage."

3. The waiver or rejection of UM/UIM coverage must demonstrate an affirmative and conscious act on the part of you, the insured.

4. UIM coverage becomes a part of every automobile liability policy by operation of law unless the insured validly waives coverage.

Adversarial Nature of UM/UIM

Most people think that when they purchase automobile insurance, their insurer will be on their side. After all, isn't this what insurance is about? Marketing slogans such as "You're in Good Hands" and "Like a Good Neighbor" reinforce this thinking and create this expectation. These marketing slogans arise from a legally recognized special type of relationship between the insured and insurer, most typically seen in the context of Personal Injury Protection (PIP) or Collision coverage.

This warm and fuzzy relationship, however, does not transfer into the UM or UIM claim processes, even though the policyholder is insured with the same insurance company.

This warm and fuzzy relationship, however, does not transfer into the UM or UIM claim processes, even though the policyholder is insured with the same insurance company. Under Washington state law, when an insured presents a UM or UIM injury claim, the rights and duties of the insurer change. With a UM or UIM claim, the law allows your insurer to stand in the shoes of the at-fault uninsured or underinsured driver. As a result, your own insurance company will no longer treat you as a good neighbor or with good hands. It is as if your insurer will represent the interests of the at-fault uninsured or underinsured driver. This is a bizarre situation that can confuse all those who are not aware of these unique and special rules.

The Supreme Court in 2001 reviewed an appeal involving an insured suing her insurer, the Hartford Company, for bad faith practices in handling her underinsured motorist claim. Specifically, the insured showed that her own automobile insurer made unreasonable settlement offers, hired an expert witness who was already retained by the at-fault party's insurer, refused to share information regarding the collision, etc. The Supreme Court ruled that the insurance company's UM/UIM relationship with its own insured is "by nature adversarial and at arm's length," and that the insurer was allowed to "be free to be adversarial within the confines of the normal rules of procedure and ethics."[4] In other words, your own insurance is allowed to fight and challenge you every step of the way.

Make Sure You Have Adequate UM/UIM Insurance and Attorney Consultation

It is not uncommon for injured parties to find themselves injured by a driver who has only Washington state's mandatory minimum insurance of $25,000 or even none at all. If you decide not to purchase any UM/UIM coverage or just at a low level, there is a risk you can be without adequate resources to protect you and your family, if you ever sustain a traumatic injury in a motor vehicle accident by the at-fault driver who has little or no liability insurance.

UM/UIM claims are complex and many legal loopholes exist for insurers to deny and limit coverage. Hiring an attorney experienced in personal injury and insurance law is often the only way to be successfully and justly compensated for your physical, emotional, and economic losses.

---

4   *Ellwein v. Hartford Company*, 142 Wn.2nd 766 (2001)

PREMISES LIABILITY

A. Slips, Trips, and Falls

Premises liability is a broad term that covers many different situations in which an individual is injured on another person's property, such as land, a building, a store, or a residence. Laws involving premises liability place a duty on property owners and businesses to provide a safe environment for people on their property.

If the property owner fails to do so and you are injured as a result, they may be held responsible for the damages caused. The injured person can pursue the same compensation they would for other types of personal injury claims for their physical, economic, and emotional losses, also known as pain and suffering (negative effects on the quality of life of the injured person).

The legal duty owed by the owner of land or occupier of a building to someone entering the premises depends on the legal classification of the injured party at the time they were hurt. The duties, responsibilities, and claims in this area of law are based on common law (common customs and practices over many, many years). These classifications include *Invitee, Licensee or Trespasser.*

If the person was on the owner's property for the purpose of business (such as going to the store, a restaurant, or doctor's office), the person is called an *Invitee.* If the person was on the property for purposes that are primarily social or familial (visiting a neighbor or attending your aunt's Christmas party), the person is called a *Licensee*. Finally, if the person was on the property without invitation or permission, the person is called a *Trespasser*.

1. Invitee: The owner or occupier of the land or structure owes the highest care to the Invitee. This requires the owner to maintain the premises in a reasonably safe condition and actively seek to discover and correct dangerous or unsafe conditions. If dangerous conditions cannot be corrected, the owner must give notice and warning to the person he/she invited onto their property to do business.

2. Social Guest or Licensee: The standard of care an owner must take for social or familial guests or Licensee is less demanding than that owed to an invitee. One must use ordinary care to repair, warn, or otherwise make reasonably safe a dangerous condition on the land, if the occupier knows or should know of the condition which poses an unreasonable risk of harm and the Licensee would not otherwise discover or appreciate the danger.

3. Trespasser: The duty to a trespasser is the least extensive, as one would expect, as the Trespasser is on the property for his own purposes without permission. The owner or occupier owes such a trespasser no duty except to refrain from willfully or wantonly injuring him.

Premises claims can arise on business properties, private residences, vacant lots, public walkways, recreational properties, and many others. Because of this, there can be various types of insurance involved, including homeowner's insurance, commercial liability coverage, self-insurance, and public entity risk management pools. When governmental properties are involved, the insured party must follow very technical laws and regulations in making a premises liability claim. When a person is injured on a business property or private residence, they will have access to a limited pool of monies to cover initial medical expenses under a "MedPay" provision (see Chapter 10 of this book

> *There can be various types of insurance involved, including homeowner's insurance, commercial liability coverage, self-insurance, and public entity risk management pools.*

on MedPay of the premises owner's insurance coverage for more discussion). Typically, MedPay provisions will provide medical coverage for $1,000, $3,000, or $5,000 of medical coverage depending on the owner's policy. Healthcare expenses over the MedPay policy limits can either be billed to the injured party's healthcare insurer or deferred until the conclusion of the liability claim.

The most commonly identified situation where people are injured and make a premises liability claim is when they trip or slip and fall inside a building or over an object leading to a building. Other instances include tripping on broken or cracked public sidewalks, on broken or poorly designed stairs or escalators, or because of defective, inadequate, or inoperative lighting, improperly maintained furniture or furnishings, fallen trees or limbs, uncovered ditches, culverts, potholes, open holes on a property, and so on.

Some of the most difficult premises claims for an injured person to successfully resolve occur when the person is injured because of the presence of a condition such as water on the floor in an aisle or bathroom, ice on the walkway leading to the door, or the infamous banana peel or other object on the grocery store floor. In those situations, the business must have noticed the dangerous condition and had the opportunity to correct it before the injured person can recover damages. The exception to this is when the owners of the business actually created the dangerous condition that caused the injury.

B. Serving Alcohol: Bars and Tavern Liability

While numerous laws and criminal sanctions have been enacted to deter those who drive while intoxicated, deterrence does not compensate those who suffer bodily harm or property damage because of a drunk driver. Drunk driving is not seasonal; it remains a major problem 365 days a year.

The law has traditionally looked for accountability from those who drink and drive. More recently, the courts have begun to recognize the chain of events leading to an injury caused by an intoxicated driver, and they may hold other parties accountable as well, such as the server or seller of the alcohol to someone who is "apparently" intoxicated.

Several years ago, the Washington State Legislature amended the law dealing with the sale of liquor to include a provision that no person

shall sell liquor to any person apparently under the influence of liquor as noted in the Alcoholic Beverage Control Act.[1] That law was interpreted by the courts in the initial cases to mean "*obviously*" intoxicated and not just "*apparently*".[2]

Obviously intoxicated v. apparently intoxicated is very significant. The "obviously intoxicated" evidence threshold is much higher and more difficult to prove. This places a greater burden on those injured by the acts of intoxicated individuals to hold accountable the business that over-served alcohol.

©iStockphoto.com/sandsun

In 2004, the Washington Supreme Court reviewed the conflict between the standard in the Alcoholic Beverage Control Act and the prior court cases (obviously intoxicated) in the landmark case of *Barrett v. Lucky Seven Saloon*.[3] In a 6-3 decision, the Washington Supreme Court Justices ruled that RCW 66.44.200(1) does set the standard for civil liability for commercial sellers of alcohol. The court expressly stated the correct standard with which to instruct a jury is the language of the statute, which is "apparent intoxication" at time of over-service of alcohol and not "obviously intoxicated." As a result, an establishment serving alcohol can be liable for injuries caused by someone they should not have served because that person was "apparently" intoxicated at the time they were provided too many drinks. The evidence does not have to establish they were "obviously intoxicated" for such service to constitute negligence on the server's part.

Two more recent cases of interest have elaborated on this area of law. The first is another significant step forward in protecting those injured by drunk drivers and those that over-serve them. In the first case, *Faust v. Albertson,* the Washington Supreme Court in 2009 dealt with a situation where there was conflicting evidence about the sobriety of an

1   Revised Code of Washington (RCW) 66.44.200 (1).

2   *Estate of Kelly By and Through Kelly v. Falin* 127 Wash.2d 31, 896 P.2d 124(1995) et al.

3   152 Wn.2d 259, 96 P 3d. 386 (2004)

individual drinking at a Moose Lodge. Patrons at the lodge, as well as the bartender, went both ways on whether he was apparently intoxicated at the time the bartender continued to serve him alcohol.

Shortly after leaving the lodge, the man drove his car head on into an oncoming car. Testing after the collision determined his blood alcohol was well over the legal limit when he caused the collision. He subsequently died a short time later, yet his blood alcohol was still over the legal limit with additional undigested alcohol in his stomach. After hearing the evidence, the jury ruled in favor of the injured plaintiff against the deceased driver, the bartender, and the lodge. An appeal of the jury's decision resulted in the Court of Appeals reversing and indicating that there was not enough direct evidence to show the apparent intoxication of the driver before he left the lodge and while he was still being served.

A final appeal was taken to the Washington Supreme Court, and they reversed the Court of Appeals decision, then reinstated the jury verdict, finding there was enough evidence to support the jury's decision. The critical components of the decision looked closely at the evidence presented for the jury's consideration. The Court found the evidence was enough to support an inference that the patron was apparently intoxicated at the time of service such that the lodge could be held accountable. The Court found the evidence sufficient in light of:

a. a combination of direct or circumstantial evidence of the patron's intoxicated appearance while being served at the lodge;

b. his "postservice" intoxicated appearance upon leaving the lodge; and

c. high blood alcohol content post-collision and in autopsy reports done shortly after the collision.

This result is consistent with the types of evidence typically used to decide cases, and our judicial system's reliance on the jury to hear the conflicting evidence, assess the reliability and credibility of the witnesses, and arrive at the truth.

The second case is a cautionary tale, and a reminder that the rules for Indian tribes can be very different because of their status as sovereign and independent nations. In *Foxworthy v. Puyallup Tribe of Indians Association*,[4] alcohol was served to a patron at an Indian casino on tribal land. The person became drunk, left the casino, and injured another motorist in a collision. The injured person then sued the tribe under Washington law for serving an apparently intoxicated person.

The Appeals Court, however, threw out the injured person's claims for injuries against the tribe, finding RCW 66.44.200 did not apply to liquor sales by the tribe. While the Puyallup Tribe had agreed to pay monies to the state based on those liquor sales, the tribe had not agreed to have state laws governing liquor sales apply to them when doing so. This case is a step back for injured persons in their efforts to obtain a fair compensation and justice when injured by a drunk driver.

As you can tell, dealing with a tribal entity, or making a claim for damages against a bar, tavern, lodge, or commercial business for over-serving a person who then drunkenly injures someone is a difficult and complex process.

C. On the Job Injuries

The Workman's Compensation Act[4] established exclusive remedies for time loss and medical care for claims by workers injured on the job, but eliminated the right of the injured worker to bring

a liability claim against his or her own employer. Compensation under the system is limited to damages such as a reduced portion of past and future income loss, the cost of retraining, treatment costs, and a small award for any permanent partial impairment, if warranted.

©iStockphoto.com/sculpies

Workman's Compensation does not pay dollar for dollar of lost income, compensate damages for the loss of quality of life (known as pain and suffering), or award full compensation for permanent injury and future care.

---

4   [5]RCW 51.40.010 et seq.

However, many people are not aware that those injured while working may have the ability to present a liability claim outside the legal limitations imposed by the Washington Workman's Compensation system.

There are two key avenues for an injured worker to recover compensation outside the statutory remedies.

The first such scenario is when the injury occurs because of the negligent, reckless, or intentional actions of *another person who is not a co-worker* or not under the direct control and supervision of the same employer, even if the injury happened on the job site. For example, an injured person who was rear-ended while working on the job is *not* prevented from making a claim against the other driver whose negligence caused the accident and caused his/her resulting injuries. In that situation, the injured party has two claims. The Department of Labor and Industries will be primarily responsible for paying the treatment bills as well as past and/or ongoing income loss. The injured party also has a negligence or liability claim against the at-fault driver for pain and suffering.

When the injury occurs because of the negligent, reckless, or intentional actions of another person who is not a co-worker or not under the direct control and supervision of the same employer.

Work-related negligence claims can also arise on construction sites, in industrial environments, or even in an office setting. The liability or negligence claim in a work setting can be against the manufacturer of a defectively or dangerously designed product, or against other sub-contractors brought in for special projects. For example, a plumber trips over an electrician's electrical cord and falls down a flight of stairs because of the unsafe placement of the cord. Here, the plumber cannot bring a claim against his employer, but he can bring a liability claim against individuals or businesses other than his employer, such as the general contractor or electrical subcontractor, for failing to provide a reasonably safe site. It is the potential of a liability claim that encourages the employment of careful workers, job safety, and compliance with safety rules.

The second type of situation wherein the injured employee may bring a liability claim directly against his or her own employer is available in only very limited circumstances. The 1998 Washington Supreme Court in *Birklid v. The Boeing Company* interpreted Workman's Compensation to establish a liability claim if there is sufficient evidence that injury resulted from the *wilful disregard* by the employer who knew and ignored the potential or actual harm to the worker. "Wilful disregard" claims made directly against the employer must be pursued through well-investigated facts and a sophisticated legal argument based in the interpretation of the law. Such claims are very difficult and success is rare.

D. Dog Bites

Dogs hold a special place in the hearts and minds of many, and have earned the well-deserved reputation as "man's best friend." Over the years, however (particularly in more urbanized communities), laws and policies have developed regarding the care and control of dogs in order to protect innocent bystanders and children.

The laws of Washington state mandate that dog owners are held responsible when their dog bites an innocent party.

Specifically, the Revised Code of Washington 16.08.040, provides for a standard of *"strict liability"* on the dog owner. The law states:

> **Liability.** The owner of any dog which shall bite any person while such person is *in or on a public place or lawfully in or on a private place including the property of the owner of such dog, shall be liable for such damages as may be suffered by the person bitten, regardless of the former viciousness of such dog* or the owner's knowledge of such viciousness. [emphasis added]

©iStockphoto.com/zudy-box

The law is straightforward and sets out a *strict liability* standard. This means that when the owner's dog bites someone else when that person is lawfully in a public place *or* on the dog owner's land, then the dog owner is liable for any injuries or damages related to the dog bite. The strict liability law holds dog owners to a higher standard of responsibility as a matter of law because of the potential for significant injury that exists when a dog bites a person.

The strict liability laws *do not* apply in all dog bite situations. For example, when there is evidence of provocation of the dog, the owner is not strictly or automatically liable for the injuries. RCW 16.08.070 of the law quoted above states:

> **Provocation as a defense.** Proof of provocation of the attack by the injured person shall be a complete defense to an action for damages.

Moreover, the strict liability statute addresses only dog bites and no other injuries occurring when a dog is involved. It differs when an owner's dog causes injury by knocking somebody to the ground. In these circumstances, the traditional common law or statutory law of negligence in Washington may apply if the judge or jury determines that the dog owner was negligent in keeping the dog under control or restraint. As stated by the Washington Supreme Court in *Arnold vs Laird*[5]:

> *The strict liability law holds dog owners to a higher standard of responsibility as a matter of law because of the potential for significant injury that exists when a dog bites a person.*

> It (is) clear a negligence cause of action arises when there is ineffective control of an animal in a situation where it would reasonably be expected that injury could occur.

Children are the victims of the majority of dog bite wounds. On average about 14 people die every year from dog attacks, and about 10 of these fatalities are children. Larger dogs like pit bulls, rottweilers, and german shepards are most commonly associated with dog bites, but it is important to remember that any dog may bite and can inflict serious bite wounds.

Here are some tips on preventing dog bites.

1. Don't pet a dog that is behind a fence, tied with a rope or chain, or in a parked car.

2. Don't try to intervene when two dogs are fighting.

---

5   [6]94 Wn. 2nd 867 (1980)

3. Don't approach stray dogs.

4. Don't stare at a dog - it may take this as a challenge.

5. Don't make sudden movements, especially towards a dog's face.

6. If a dog is with its owner, always ask if it's all right to pet the dog.

If you, your child or someone you know is attacked by a dog:

1. Try to block the dog from biting by allowing it to chew on your backpack, jacket, or anything else other than yourself.

2. If knocked down, curl into a ball and wrap your arms around your head and neck to protect them.

3. Seek medical attention from a doctor; don't treat the wound yourself. Even what appears to be a minor bite wound can have serious consequences as there could be severe tissue damage under the skin from the dog's teeth. The wound could easily become infected.

4. Ask your child for any information he/she can remember about the dog. Rabies is rarely transmitted by dogs as vaccination is common, but there is always a possibility of this fatal disease. If the dog is located, its vaccine history can and should be checked.

5. Report the bite to Animal Control.

6. Seek a consultation from experienced legal counsel.

BICYCLES AND TRAUMATIC INJURIES

CHAPTER 16

Bicycles have become quite popular over the past few years. With increasing gas prices, more and more folks ride to and from work or use bikes to run errands. It is a convenient and inexpensive method of travel and a fun way to exercise by yourself or with family or friends.

Many cities have recognized the increase in bike traffic and have constructed special bike lanes. Parks have made trails accessible to cyclists. Unfortunately, some automobile drivers do not respect the bicyclists' rights to share the roads. Equally important, some bicyclists have not been educated on how to legally and safely share the roads with automobiles, resulting in serious and sometimes fatal injuries.

©iStockphoto.com/Mario Savoia

Did you know:

1. Nearly 1 million children are injured each year in bicycle-related collisions.

2. A bicyclist is fatally injured every 6 hours.

3. 49 percent of all bicycle fatalities occurred to children under the age of 16.

4. While bicycle v. vehicle collisions only account for one-third of all collisions, they account for a majority of the catastrophic injuries.

The most common causes of bicycle v. motor vehicle collisions occur when:

1. The motor vehicle driver opens his/her driver's door when parked;

2. A motor vehicle sideswipes a bicyclist while passing;

3. A motorist fails to yield the right of way to the cyclist;

4. The cyclist travels over a road surface hazard.

Though a cyclist has as much of a right to the roadway as a motor vehicle in Washington,[1] the number and types of bicyclist v. motor vehicle collisions that occur seem to indicate that motor vehicle drivers are not aware of cyclists' road rights.

Here are a few common examples of when cars and bicycles crash.

Driver Opens Door of a Parked Car

Cyclists are required to ride as far to the right of the road as possible. This places a cyclist close to parked cars. There is a duty for a person opening a door of a parked car not to do so unless it is safe to other cars passing as well as cyclists. A traumatic injury caused by the opening of a parked car door is generally the fault of the door opener.

Sideswiped by a Passing Motor Vehicle

Another rule of the road for a motorist requires him/her to maintain a safe space while passing a bicyclist. The problem of sufficient passing space has become more complicated as more trucks, buses, and super-sized SUVs are on the roadway.

A vehicle traveling behind a cyclist who wants to pass him/her cannot do so unless it is clearly safe. This may require the busy motorist to slow down and wait until there is enough space to pass or to change lanes. It is not uncommon following a collision of this type for the at-fault party's insurance company to argue that the cyclist was not as far to the right as he/she could have or should have been. The appropriate counter-argument to this claim is that the motorist had a duty to wait

While bicycle v. vehicle collisions only account for one-third of all collisions, they account for a majority of the catastrophic injuries.

1   See RCW 46.61.755

until it was safe to pass, and that knocking a cyclist over is not a permissible option, despite the urgency of the motorist to pass.

A bicyclist is fatally injured every 6 hours.

Turning Into the Path of the Cyclist

It is most common for motor vehicle v. bicycle collision to occur when the motor vehicle turns into the path of a cyclist. In this situation the motorist is liable for the collision in light of a basic rule of the road — a vehicle may not turn unless it is safe to do so.

Common Roadway Hazards for a Cyclist

Roadway hazards (pot holes, sewer grates, slick paint, improperly placed monuments or manhole covers, and disruptions to the road surface from street construction work) are particularly dangerous for a cyclist as they may cause cyclists to lose control or veer into the path of another vehicle. These types of personal injury claims are complicated and involve taking action against the governmental or public agency that maintains the roadway. It is important to note that filing a claim against any public agency is coupled with special requirements and time limits before a lawsuit may proceed.

What to Do After a Bicycle Collision

The checklist below sets out what you need to do as a cyclist if you are ever involved in a bicycle collision, especially one in which you receive traumatic personal injuries:

Here are a few common examples of when cars and bicycles crash:

> *Driver opens door of a parked car.*
>
> *Sideswiped by a passing motor vehicle.*
>
> *Turning into the path of the cyclist.*
>
> *Common roadway hazards for a cyclist.*

1. **Call Police**: Both the cyclist and the motorist have a legal obligation to report the collision to the police if there is any physical injury or property damage, and to remain at the scene of the collision until police arrive.

2. **Exchange Information with the Driver**: Both cyclists and motorists have a legal obligation to exchange information at the scene of the accident including

their names, addresses, phone numbers, driver's license numbers, license plate numbers, make of car, and automobile insurance policy numbers.

3. **Obtain Names and Phone Numbers of Any Witnesses**: Witnesses to the collision and the injuries can be helpful in documenting what happened and recording the information you need.

4. **Obtain the Police Collision Report Number**: Before the police leave the collision scene, ask for a card from the officer and write down the collision report number.

5. **Write Down How the Collision Happened**: Soon after the collision, draw a detailed map or diagram using arrows to show the position and direction of yourself and all motor vehicles involved.

6. **Seek Medical Attention**: Consult a doctor immediately for an assessment of your physical condition and treatment of any personal injuries from the collision.

7. **Contact the Insurance Company of the Driver**: It is important to notify the insurance company of the driver of the vehicle for two reasons: first, to find out if the driver carried Personal Injury Protection (PIP) coverage, which would be available to pay the cyclist's medical bills and provide other benefits; second, to notify them of a possible third party or liability claim against the driver for causing the injuries and damages in the collision.

8. **Contact Your Auto Insurance Company**: Even though you are on a bicycle, you have PIP coverage available from the driver's PIP and your PIP coverage.

9. **Preserve Evidence**: Take photographs of any visible injuries to you, damage to your bicycle, and/or roadway hazards that caused or contributed to your injuries, if any. Keep any damaged clothing and bike parts. Get a written assessment of the damage to your bicycle. If possible, avoid having the bike repaired until any issues of liability and damages from the collision are concluded.

Notice how these practical tips are very similar to the list of what to do in any type of motor vehicle collision. No one plans on having a traumatic injury in a car or on a bicycle, but that doesn't mean you shouldn't be prepared.

CONSORTIUM CLAIMS

One of the least understood components of personal injury claims arising out of traumatic injury is the "loss of consortium" claim, most often associated with a spouse's loss of physical intimacy.

In fact, loss of consortium is broader than the spousal relationship, encompassing spouses and children. It is based in the recognition that damage occurs when the family's normal functioning is disrupted because of an injury to one of its members.

A. Husband-Wife Relationship

Loss of consortium is a claim separate from the claims of the physically injured person. The 1980 Washington Supreme Court said in *Lungren v. Whitney's Inc.* that either spouse may seek compensation from loss of society, affection, assistance, and conjugal fellowship, as well as loss or impairment of sexual relationships when the other is injured by the negligence of a third party. Under current law, the person making a loss of consortium claim must be married to the injured person at the time of the traumatic occurrence.

B. Parent-Child Relationship

Health care providers treating those with traumatic injury have long known that injuries or deaths

©PhotoAlto Photography/Veer

impact every aspect of family interaction. Both the Washington legislature and courts recognized this when they expanded the consortium claim to include both sides of the parent-child relationship.

The legislature did so in two key statutory provisions. Revised Code of Washington (RCW) 4.22.020 first allowed children to obtain loss of consortium damages for being deprived of their parent's love, care, companionship, and guidance. RCW 4.24.010 includes the parent's loss of consortium of a child who was killed by the negligence of another in the definition of those who may make a consortium claim. The parent's loss is defined as the services, support, love, and companionship of the child and the destruction of the parent-child relationship.

In 1984, the Washington State Supreme Court in *Veland v. Pengo Hydra-Pull Corp.* gave the children of an injured but surviving parent the same right to obtain compensation for the losses of the parent-child relationship. In doing so, the court noted that:

> Although a monetary award may be a poor substitute for the loss of a parent's society and companionship, it is the only workable way that our legal system has found to ease the injured party's tragic loss.

The underlying rationale for the claim is supported by both research and common life experience. When a spouse and/or parent is physically unable to perform his or her usual and customary activities of daily living, the entire family is impacted. The roles within the family are changed. Many times members are uncomfortable with the change or new roles. The uninjured spouse and/or children are called upon to undertake tasks and responsibilities, both in and out of the home, which they are unaccustomed to and may be unprepared to perform. For example, sometimes the uninjured spouse and/or child must themselves become the caregiver for the one they have relied on for much of their own care in the past. This results in frustration and anger that is often unrecognized and untreated.

The research in this area has been most extensive in situations of brain trauma and persons with disabilities. It is clear that traumatic injuries and chronic disabilities create distinct stressors on family members and result in marked disruption of family functioning. The occurrence of Post Traumatic Stress Disorder (PTSD) has also been identified in surviving family members in the context of traumatically caused death.

IMPAIRMENT AND DISABILITY CLAIMS

CHAPTER 18

Most people recover sufficiently from traumatic injury to return to work. For some, however, traumatic injury leaves them disabled from working for periods of time, or even permanently.

The term disability can mean different things to different people. In the context of a personal injury case a distinction is first made between an *impairment* and a *disability*.

Let's start by understanding impairments. An impairment rating is a measurement of the loss of joint motion and structural integrity of a joint of the body. It is significant deviation, loss, or loss of use of any body structure or body function in an individual with a traumatic injury or health condition. An impairment is independent of a person's age, gender, occupation, or socioeconomic status. An impairment can be observed and measured uniformly and have the same result when different doctors evaluate you. Interestingly, an impairment or loss of joint motion often carries pain with it and may even lead to a disability. However, this is not always true.

Indeed/Photodisc/Getty Images

Some people can have an impairment from a loss of joint motion, yet remain fully functional in regards to their employment and function in society and have no disability. For example, amputation of a pinky is certainly an impairment because of the loss of joint motion of one finger. However, it may not create a disability when it happens to a customer service phone operator. But that same amputation to a concert pianist would create an impairment and perhaps a disability as well.

A *disability* from a traumatic injury results from a reduction in your ability to participate actively at work in a manner consistent with your age, gender, and socioeconomic status when compared to pre-trauma function. A disability limits your ability to perform tasks because of your injury and limits your ability to compete in the open job market. Pain from an underlying injury may be related to your disability, but pain itself does not influence an impairment rating.

> *An impairment rating is a measurement of the loss of joint motion and structural integrity of a joint of the body.*

Impairment rating systems come in many forms, but the one most insurers recognize in their evaluation of money damages for traumatic injuries is the *American Medical Association's Guides to the Evaluation of Permanent Impairment*, now in its 6th edition (2008). If you have an injury to a joint that reduces its strength and motion, then it is critical for your case to have your doctor provide an impairment rating. This will have an important impact on the value of your case. If your doctor does not know how to conduct this type of evaluation, then have him/her refer you to another provider who does.

A. Disability Benefits

If your traumatic injury interferes or limits your ability to perform your normal work, family commitments, and daily activities as identified in writing by your doctor, then you likely have a disability. The length of the disability and its scope is determined by your doctor. If you have a disability, then it is important to understand three potential financial safety nets. We previously discussed wage loss insurance benefits under your PIP coverage, if your disability is from a motor vehicle collision. Please review Chapter 9, "Insurance — Personal Injury Protection (PIP)" at pages 25–30.

The other two safety nets include:

* Private Disability Insurance Policies

* Social Security Disability Insurance (SSDI) and/or Supplemental Security Income (SSI)

B. Private Disability Insurance Policies

Many employers provide Short and/or Long-Term Disability coverage in addition to regular sick-leave and vacation pay. Many individuals, particularly those who are self-employed, purchase individual disability policies to meet their specific needs. Though generally providing similar coverage, disability policies vary widely in specifics.

There are two general types of private disability policies:

* Short-Term Disability (STD) and
* Long-Term Disability (LTD)

These policies are often purchased together and are intended to dovetail to provide continuity of benefits. Most Short Term Disability policies have a waiting period before benefits begin, usually a maximum of 14 days after onset of a disability. These policies then cover a portion of the wage earner's income for a specified period, from several months but not longer than two years. Usually this period is only until the policyholder becomes eligible for benefits under a Long-Term Disability policy. LTD policies usually have a waiting period of a few weeks to several months. This is called the "elimination period." A common elimination period is ninety days."

Disability policies generally provide for payment of 40 to 70 percent of the policyholder's income, tax-free. Providing less than 100 percent benefit is thought to give the policyholder incentive to return to work, if possible.

To qualify for benefits under a disability policy, the claimant/policyholder must meet the contract definition of "disability." There are three general categories of policy definitions; the differences are significant:

1. **Own Occupation:** This is the highest level of coverage provided under disability policies and is becoming increasingly rare in the industry. Disability under this type of contract is generally defined as:

    The inability to perform the material and substantial duties of your regular occupation. The insurance company will consider your occupation to be the occupation you were engaged in at the time you became disabled and will pay the claim even if you are working in some other capacity.

2. **Income Replacement:** This has become the most common policy definition. Most disability insurers have stopped offering Own Occupation coverage and have replaced the definition with Income Replacement, which usually states:

> Because of sickness or injury you are unable to perform the material and substantial duties of your occupation and are not engaged in any other occupation.

3. **Gainful Occupation Coverage:** This definition gives the insurer the broadest discretion in determining disability and is a very common definition in employer-sponsored policies. This definition provides:

> Because of sickness or injury you are unable to perform the material and substantial duties of your occupation, or any occupation for which you are deemed reasonably qualified by education, training and experience.

> Since there is a substantial difference between the insurer's potential pay-out under each of these definitions, there is also a difference in the premiums charged for each. When purchasing a disability policy, the least costly policies will invariably use the Gainful Occupation definition, effectively rendering the policy nearly useless *unless the policyholder is completely unable to do any work of any type or pay level.*

Coordination of claims arising out of a traumatic injury is an important aspect of legal representation of a person with a disability.

The majority of conflict and litigation under disability policies arises from these insurance contract definitions. Employer-provided disability policies are subject to the Employee Retirement Income Security Act (ERISA). This is a federal law that sets standards for employer-based health and pension plans. ERISA is a complex law which, in part, governs how litigation around disability policy disputes must be handled. When a conflict arises between you and a disability insurer, it would be very wise to promptly consult with an attorney versed in ERISA requirements.

Disability and insurance laws are complex and are frequently changing. If you have been injured and are unable to return to work as directed by your doctor, then you should seek consultation with an attorney knowledgeable about long-term injuries, insurance claims, and personal injury and disability laws in order to protect their access to healthcare and income benefits.

C. Social Security Disability Insurance

If you have a traumatic injury that prevents you from returning to work and limits your abilities to participate in your regular activities, then the first place to look for long-term support is your private disability policy. If you do not have a private disability policy, then you are left to unscramble state and federal benefits programs.

The largest of the federal disability programs is administered by the Social Security Administration (SSA).

The Social Security Administration administers two primary programs for persons with disabilities. The Social Security Disability Insurance (SSDI) program covers those individuals who are considered "insured" by virtue of having worked a certain period of time and paid into the social security system before becoming disabled (Title II of the Social Security Act). Supplemental Security Income (SSI) provides benefits to disabled persons based on financial need. While both share some common requirements and features, each covers somewhat different situations.

1. **Social Security Disability Insurance** is available to individuals who have worked a certain amount of time prior to becoming disabled. Certain disabled dependents of the insured worker may also be eligible for these benefits. Eligibility for SSDI depends on the disabled person's status as an insured under the program and does not consider the individual's income or resources.

2. **Supplemental Security Income** benefits (Title XVI of the Social Security Act) provide payments to individuals (including children under age 18) who are disabled and have limited income and resources.

For both programs, the definition of disability is the same. The law defines disability as:

> The inability to engage in any substantial gainful activity (SGA) by reason of a *medically determinable physical or mental impairment(s)* which can be expected to result in death or which has lasted or can be expected to last for a continuous period of not less than 12 months.

A "medically determinable impairment" is defined as a condition that can be confirmed by medically accepted methods. Your doctor must document the diagnosis, reasons for the diagnosis, and whether improvement of the condition can be expected. An impairment cannot be based solely on your report of symptoms and limitations.

3. **The Process**

Processing of initial claims is usually done through Social Security field offices and state agencies, usually called Disability Determination Services (DDS). The field offices usually handle the non-medical aspects of an application, while the DDS handles the medical aspects and makes decisions on whether the claimant is disabled under the law.

To apply for either SSDI or SSI, you must submit an application for benefits. This can be done online (www.socialsecurity.gov), over the phone, or in person at a field office. The application asks for general personal information, work history, and medical information. Once the application is complete, the Disability Determination Service will request information from your doctor(s) to determine if you are disabled under the SSA's definition. It often takes three to five months to receive an initial determination of eligibility.

Disability Determination Services are state agencies funded by the federal government. The DDS is responsible for obtaining medical information and making the initial determination about whether you are or are not disabled under the law. The DDS usually attempts to make the disability determination based on your treating doctors' records. However, if a determination cannot be made on that information, the DDS may arrange for a consultative examination through your doctor or through one chosen by the DDS.

Once the medical information is received, the determination of disability is made by a two-person team consisting of a medical or psychological consultant and a disability examiner. The team can also make a determination that you are an appropriate candidate for vocational rehabilitation and can refer you to the state vocational rehabilitation agency. Once the team has made the determination on the application, it is sent back to the field office for action.

If the DDS determines that you fit the criteria for disability, assuming all other eligibility requirements are met, the field office will compute the benefit amount and begin paying benefits. Only about 40 percent of initial applications are allowed at this stage.

If the DDS determines that you do not meet the criteria, the field office will advise you of this and of your right to appeal the decision. On a first request to reconsider the decision, the application and any additional information is returned to the DDS for re-evaluation by a different two-person decision-making team.

If the claim is again denied, you can appeal again. The second appeal is processed through a Hearing Office within the SSA's Office of Hearings and Appeals. An Administrative Law Judge (ALJ) makes the decision on this appeal, usually after receiving additional medical information and holding a hearing.

The final stage of the administrative appeal process, if you are again denied by the Office of Hearings and Appeals, is to file an appeal with the Appeals Council. You generally have only sixty days to appeal at this level.

If you wish to pursue benefits after completing the appeal process within the SSA, you may file a civil suit in Federal District Court. Most appeals are completed well before filing such a suit.

4. How Does the SSA Decide Eligibility?

The SSA uses a five-step "sequential evaluation process" to determine eligibility for benefits. This process requires review of your current work activity, severity of impairments, residual functional capacity, past work history, age, education, and work experience. Evaluation progresses from one step to the next.

1). Is the claimant working?

If you are working and earn more than a specified amount ($900 per month in 2007), you will not be considered disabled.

If the claimant is not working, go to Step 2.

2). Is the condition "severe"?

The condition must interfere with basic work-related activities for a claim to be considered. If it does not, you will not be considered disabled and not eligible for benefits.

If the condition does interfere with basic work-related activities, go to Step 3.

3). Is the condition found in the list of disabling conditions?

For each of the major body systems, the SSA maintains a list of medical conditions that are so severe that they are automatically considered disabling. If your condition is not on the list, then the condition is evaluated to determine if it so severe that it causes a comparable level of impairment. If it does not, you are not considered disabled and are not eligible. If the condition is severe, got to Step 4.

4). Can the claimant do the work he or she did previously?

If a condition is severe but not at the same level of severity as a medical condition on the list, then SSA will determine if the condition interferes with your ability to do the work you did previously. If it does not, the claim will be denied. If it does, go to Step 5.

5). Can you do any other type of work?

If you cannot do the work you did in the past, SSA will

determine whether you are able to make adjustments and perform a different job. The SSA considers your medical conditions, age, education, past work experience, and any transferable skills. If the claimant cannot adjust to other work, the claim will be approved. If you can adjust to other work, the claim will be denied.

Disability benefits for workers and widows usually cannot begin for five months after the onset of the disability. If awarded, benefits will be paid beginning the sixth full month after the date the disability began. SSI benefits may begin as early as the first full month after the individual applied for or became eligible for benefits. Under SSI, benefits may be paid during the period in which a formal disability determination is made. If you are found ineligible, the government may require you to pay back the benefits paid during this period.

Other Benefits

Medicare or Medicaid benefits may be available to individuals covered by SSDI or SSI. Medicare provides benefits for medical care for those over age 65 or who are eligible for SSDI and have been receiving benefits for twenty-four months. Medicaid is a medical benefit program administered by the individual states (the term Medicaid is used in many but not all states). It usually covers those eligible for SSI benefits. Eligibility rules vary from state to state. In Washington, the Medicaid program is administered by the Department of Social and Health Services (www1.dshs.wa.gov).

Coordination of claims and benefits arising out of a traumatic injury is a vital aspect of legal representation of a person with a long-term disability. The laws are complex and frequently changing.

Patients who have been injured by the negligence of another and left with a potential disability should seek consultation with an attorney knowledgeable about long-term injuries, insurance claims, and personal injury and disability laws in order to protect their access to healthcare and income benefits.

Wrongful Death

CHAPTER 19

If a person dies due to the negligence of another party, the relatives of the deceased may be able to recover compensation for their loved one's "wrongful death." This should be a straightforward principle, but in Washington, the laws are messy, confusing, and can be unfair to certain family members.

For example, the wrongful death laws in Washington are contained in five separate statutes that set forth the type of legal actions that can be raised in negligence-related death. Two of the statutes are referred to as the "wrongful death" statutes,[1] and the other three are known as "survival" statutes.[2]

It is critical to note that a full understanding of these complex laws is difficult and any individual with a potential wrongful death claim should seek legal counsel as soon as they can do so.

Wrongful Death Statutes

The damages under the wrongful death statutes (known as the "statutory beneficiaries") are held by a spouse, children under 18, and dependents. They can claim the tangible money and income (the

---

1   RCW 4.20.010 and 4.20.020
2   RCW 4.20.046, 4.20.060, 4.24.010

RICHARD H. ADLER
Attorney at Law, Adler Giersch PS

law uses the phrase "pecuniary losses") the deceased would have provided to the beneficiaries, and the intangible loss of the support, services, love, affection, care, companionship, society, and consortium.

The damages under the wrongful death statutes (known as the "statutory beneficiaries") are held by a spouse, children under 18, and dependents.

If there is no spouse, children under 18, or other dependents, then the personal representative of the estate is empowered to bring an action for the benefit of the deceased's parents and siblings if they were dependent upon the deceased for financial support. Natural children born outside the marriage also qualify as statutory beneficiaries. Under present law, an unmarried partner living with the decedent or the estranged spouse who did not intend to resume the marital relationship prior to death are excluded as statutory beneficiaries. Court decisions continue to evolve around this subject area.

Pursuant to RCW 4.20.010, the right and power to bring a lawsuit for losses sustained by statutory beneficiaries of the deceased is reserved exclusively to the personal representative (the administrator or executor) of the estate of the deceased. This can be a confusing part of the law because the person(s) who suffer(s) injury as a result of negligent death of a loved one may not be the same person empowered to bring a wrongful death lawsuit. For example, the surviving spouse of the deceased is not empowered to bring the lawsuit unless she is also the executrix (the administrative or personal representative) of her husband's estate. By the same token, the surviving children or parents of the deceased must depend upon the personal representative of the estate as the named party to prosecute their claims. Many times when tragedy strikes, there may be no will, and therefore no personal representative of the estate. This situation can be remedied by filing legal papers seeking the appointment of a personal representative (who may be a surviving family member or a statutory beneficiary).

One of the advantages of having the personal representative of the deceased's estate as the named party in the lawsuit is that any monetary damages recovered do not become the assets of the estate of the decedent and cannot be used to satisfy the debts of the estate.

Survival Statutes

The remaining three statutes are commonly called the "survival" statutes.[3] They are so named because the legal claim survives the death of the person, allowing a lawsuit to be filed as if the person had not died.

"Wrongful death" actions and "survivor" actions pursuant to the "general survival" statute (RCW 4.20.046) are fundamentally different. Wrongful death actions allow for the surviving spouse and dependent beneficiaries to recover damages they suffer as a result of the death of the decedent. On the other hand, the personal representative may prosecute claims the decedent would have had if he or she had not died. In other words, the personal representative can bring a lawsuit for money damages and obligations owed to the decedent, as well as for the suffering the decedent experienced before death. In the context of death claims, the general survival statute (RCW 4.20.046) provides for the additional measure of damages for the "pain and suffering, anxiety, emotional distress, or humiliation personal to and suffered by the deceased."

Like the wrongful death statutes, claims brought under the general survivorship statute may only be prosecuted by the personal representative. However, the damages recovered pursuant to the survivorship statutes are the property of the estate of the deceased and are subject to the debts of the estate.

RCW 4.20.060 is commonly called the "special survivor statute." It allows for the recovery of the same pre-death pain and suffering damages as allowed for in the general survivor statute (RCW 4.20.046), but the monies recovered go directly to the statutory beneficiaries and do not become the property of the estate, and are not reachable by the estate's creditors. Once again, this legal distinction illustrates the importance of involving legal representation to decide whether to file a wrongful death, general survivor, or special survivor type of action. This will depend on many factors, including the identity of statutory beneficiaries, protection of surviving family members, and balancing the needs between the beneficiaries and the estate.

Finally, according to the second "special survivor" statute, RCW 4.24.010, parents are entitled to bring a direct action (no requirement

---

3   RCW 4.20.046, 4.20.060, and 4.24.010

for a personal representative) for the wrongful death or injury to a minor child, or a child upon whom they are dependent for support. This includes the loss of a viable unborn child. Damages that may be recovered include medical expenses, loss of love and companionship, and injury to or destruction of the parent-child relationship. Each parent is entitled to claim damages for loss of love and companionship and damage to or destruction of the parent-child relationship. Once again, these damages are the property of the beneficiaries and are not reachable by creditors of the child's estate. Notice that the surviving parents of an adult child must be dependent on that individual to be a "special survivor." Merely being close emotionally is not enough under current Washington law.

Statute of Limitations

The Statute of Limitations is a law defining the time limit within which a legal action must be commenced before the right to prosecute certain claims is lost forever. See Chapter 29, pages 110–113. Generally, personal injury actions are governed by the three-year Statute of Limitations. However, there are legal traps in the area of wrongful death laws, since they contain limitations that can range from one to three years, depending on the legal theories of recovery. Another complexity of the wrongful death Statute of Limitations concerns minor children (less than 18 years old) who are related to the deceased. Generally, the Statute of Limitations for those under 18 years in most personal injury actions does not expire until three years after they reach the age of majority (18 years). However, in wrongful death claims, the three-year clock ticks the same for adult beneficiaries as it does for minor beneficiaries.

Final Thought

Because of the complexities of the statutes governing wrongful death actions, the issues of timely actions to open estates and initiate litigation to avoid Statute of Limitation problems, and the expertise required to successfully prosecute death claims, individuals are encouraged to seek the assistance of experienced legal counsel as soon after the negligent death of a loved one as they can reasonably manage.

NEGLIGENCE AND LIABILITY

CHAPTER 20

In law, a claim for damages caused by another's actions is called a "tort." A tort is simply a civil, as opposed to criminal, wrong for which a remedy (money) may be obtained. The wrong committed is generally a careless or negligent act.

The determination of who is at-fault dictates who pays for the consequences. The person at-fault is legally responsible for the injuries and damages of anyone hurt by that person's negligence.

To bring a claim against another person, the person's careless or negligent act must be the cause of the injured party's damages. The at-fault party is called the "liable" party. The determination of who is at-fault dictates who pays for the consequences. The person at-fault is legally responsible for the injuries and damages of anyone hurt by that person's negligence. However, an injured person must establish *four* essential elements in the claim:

1. The person who caused the traumatic injury had a legal duty to avoid the actions that led to the injury, e.g., the person had a duty to stop at a stop sign;

2. The person who caused the traumatic injury did not fulfill that legal duty (attorneys refer to this as the "breach" of legal duty), e.g., the person failed to stop at the stop sign;

3. The traumatic event was caused by breach of the duty; and

4. Traumatic injuries and related physical, economic, and psychological/emotional damages resulted.

RICHARD H. ADLER
Attorney at Law, Adler Giersch PS

Fault is established based on the individual facts that are applied to long-standing laws, rules, or regulations. For example, when a driver runs a stoplight, rear-ends another, or crosses the center line while driving, fault is seemingly obvious. But what if one driver rear-ends another because the lead driver suddenly stopped or had defective brake lights? What if a driver crosses the center line because a driver to the right changed lanes into his? The issue of liability or fault takes into account all the circumstances.

Where liability is in question, extensive gathering and understanding of the facts is necessary to determine which person or persons are at fault. These facts include not only the statements of each party involved, observations of witnesses, and opinions of police and investigators, but also evidence at the scene of a collision (such as skid marks, distances, point of impact to the vehicles, point of final rest of each vehicle, severity of impact, etc.).

There are times, however, when the evaluation of all the available details is not enough. These instances require evaluation by experts in the field in which the liability questions arise, such as engineers and specially trained collision reconstructionists who can use principles of math, physics, and engineering to reconstruct the incident.

There are also situations in which more than one person is responsible. For instance, when one car pulls out of a driveway in front of another, the car that pulled out may be solely liable for failing to yield the right of way to an oncoming car. However, if the oncoming car was speeding, that driver may be held partially liable since the excessive speed may have contributed to the crash. These situations present issues of "comparative negligence."

In Washington State, if two or more people are at fault, each can make a claim against the other for their portion of liability. For example, if Driver B is 100 percent liable for a collision and Driver A incurred $1,000 in medical expenses as a result, Driver A could recover the full $1,000 from Driver B. However, if Driver A is 25 percent at fault, he or she can make a claim against Driver B for only 75 percent of his or her damages, or $750.

Determining who is at fault is one of the first steps in evaluating a traumatic injury. Though sometimes clear, this can be an involved and complicated process, and is the fundamental basis of a personal injury claim.

When dealing with insurance companies or the court process, proof is what matters most. Never assume that the insurance company that is responsible to pay the claim for the at-fault party will simply do so.

The at-fault party's insurer will always try to point the finger at someone else or something else; they always look for a way not to pay.

Even when fault is clear, expect the insurance company to maintain their defense every step of the way. Insurers require that premiums be paid on time, yet they are slow to accept responsibility and even slower to reasonably compensate the one with a traumatic injury claim.

Independent Medical Examination (IME) — Is it Really "Independent"?

CHAPTER 21

"The business of insurance is one affected by the public interest, requiring that all persons be actuated by good faith, abstain from deception, and practice honesty and equity in all insurance matters. Upon the insurer, the insured, the providers, and the representatives rest the duty of preserve inviolate the integrity of insurance.[1]"

Does the insurer really "act in good faith, abstain from deception and practice honesty and equity"? What about "Independent" Medical Examinations (IMEs)? Companies tell their injured insureds that their medical examinations will be conducted by an independent examiner. They sometimes claim the evaluation is sought because they are "concerned" about their insured's health and want to make sure that the treatment is effective in resolving injuries. However, the reality of the IME is quite different. It is nick-named an "Insurance Medical Examination" or "Involuntary Medical Examination." Attorneys representing those with traumatic injuries know that many, many of these examiners are simply hired guns, and their job is to find a way in which the insurer does not have to pay for treatment expenses.

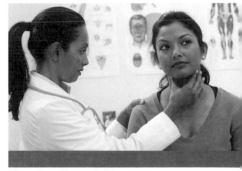

©Image Source Photography/Veer

---

1   RCW 48.01.030

The auto insurer does more than *request* their insured attend an IME. They *compel* the examination under the terms of the insurance policy with their insured, which typically states:

> A person making a claim *shall* be examined by any physician *we choose* and *paid by us* as often as we reasonably may require. (Emphasis added).

The PIP Insurance Medical Exam can have a toxic effect on many aspects of your health care recovery and personal injury claim.

In order to continue receiving PIP benefits, the injured party must comply with the terms and conditions of his/her insurance contract. The patient is placed in a lose-lose position. If they attend the IME, treatment will be predictably terminated by the hired-gun doctor. If they do not attend the IME, PIP benefits will terminate because of their failure to cooperate with the terms of the insurance policy requiring attendance at the IME when requested. The insurer will also withhold payment of treatment bills until the insured attends the IME. After the IME report is issued, the insurer will deny payment when their doctor predictably states that treatment was not necessary and/or related to the collision (remember, this is not an independent examination, no matter how many times the insurance company uses the word).

The true purpose of the IME is cost-containment, a purposeful effort to reduce the amount of benefits paid out for care under the PIP policy. When the insurer sets up the examination, hand-picks the examiner, and pays the examiner or agency a significant fee, a negative outcome for the patient is often a given. In essence, the insurer gets what it pays for, and you do not.

The PIP Insurance Medical Exam can have a toxic effect on many aspects of your health care recovery and personal injury claim. When an insurer stops payment of bills, you will be required to pay the doctor or health care provider out of pocket. Most folks do not have that amount of money. This may result in the injured party's condition getting worse. The IME report can unsettle a patient's confidence in his/her own doctor. The IME examiners' report will be used to challenge the reasonableness and necessity of care, and/or can be used to challenge whether the treatment is related to the trauma. It also often resurfaces during settlement negotiations with the liability insurer or the underinsured motorist insurer, creating obstacles for a fair and reasonable settlement without the cost and burden of going to court.

Despite the obstacles presented by a pending IME, you are not powerless if you seek legal consultation before the IME occurs.

Actions can be taken to help level the playing field and restore good faith and honesty to the IME process.

This requires consideration of the following:

1. Only the patient, through his/her attorney, has the legal right to intervene and effectively challenge the insurer's need for the examination, selection of the examiner, and parameters of the evaluation. From a legal point of view, more can be done to protect a patient's legal rights and access to health care *prior* to an IME than after it.

2. Experienced personal injury attorneys will insist the insurer follow the dictates of Washington Administration Code (WAC) 284-30-395, which requires an insurer to select an examiner that is "currently licensed, certified, or registered to practice in the same health field or specialty as the health care professional that treated the insured." The intent of this code provision is to safeguard the patient/insured's choice of health care provider. For example, a PIP insurer may no longer request a medical doctor to evaluate chiropractic care or vice versa. This means that only a chiropractor can evaluate the necessity of the chiropractic care, a medical doctor can only evaluate the necessity of the medical care, and so on.

3. The "gold standard" for attorneys representing individuals subjected to an IME requires the attorney to exercise their legal right to be present during the IME. An attorney's presence at the IME oversees that the procedures, tests, and results are reported accurately and ensures that the appointment does not become an interrogation of the insured. Experienced counsel will also

audiotape the examination to eliminate the "recollection" contest between the patient and the examiner during settlement as to what was and was not said during the examination.

4. When an IME takes place and an adverse opinion is provided by the examiner that limits or terminates your health care treatment, it is important for your treating doctor to obtain a copy of the report. You have a legal right to obtain a copy under WAC 284-30-395. You request the IME report from your insurance company, not the IME doctor. Once the IME report is in hand, it must be carefully read and responded to by the treating doctor. This response will rebut erroneous, inconsistent, or incomplete findings and conclusions, provide the findings which support ongoing injury requiring care, state the ongoing relationship of the injuries/conditions to the traumatic incident, and specify what additional care is required to move the patient toward maximum medical improvement.

An injured party working together with his/her lawyer form the first line of defense from debilitating physical injury, financial loss, and the cost-containment practices of the insurance companies. Working together, the attorney and client can make insurance companies take seriously their duty to "Act in good faith, abstain from deception and practice honesty and equity."

PAPER REVIEWS OF MEDICAL RECORDS

CHAPTER 22

In addition to IMEs, insurance companies seeking to reduce payments under the PIP policy have other cost-containment strategies, including PIP Paper Reviews, also known as a Peer Review. This is when an insurance company gets a medical opinion about an injured person's treatment without the patient ever being examined in person.

The insurance company simply sends the injured party's health care records to a doctor to review and pass judgment on the insured's condition and treatment needs.

The insurance company's doctor is supposed to review all the records sent. Sometimes the records sent are incomplete and leave out important information. A peer review or paper-review doctor will look for several elements, such as: conditions that pre-existed the trauma; treatment outside a very contained time frame; treatment he/she finds unreasonable or unnecessary; and/or failure of your doctor to document certain specifics that would support continued care.

Once a Peer or Paper Review is completed, the PIP insurance company will often discontinue benefits based on the reviewer's

©iStockphoto.com/ Rudyanto Wijaya

A Paper Review, also known as a Peer Review, is when an insurance company gets a medical opinion about an injured person's treatment without the patient ever being examined in person.

opinion. As with an IME, this opinion can affect the injured party's ability to continue to receive PIP health care benefits and obtain continued health care.

"Proximate Cause" Attacks

Insurance companies are well-versed in finding ways to poke holes in claims and minimize payments. One of the primary ways in which a claim can be attacked is with the use of the legal principal of "proximate cause."

Proximate cause means:

> A cause which in a direct sequence [unbroken by any new independent cause] produces the injury complained of and without which such injury would not have happened. (Washington Pattern Jury Instructions 15.01)

©iStockphoto.com/Nemanja Pesic

This simply means that the negligent event (car collision, fall, malpractice) on which the claim is made must be the direct cause of the traumatic injury. While such connection may seem obvious to the injured party, there are many approaches an insurer will use or abuse to discount the full extent of the traumatic injuries. Many of the insurer's proximate cause attacks fall into predictable patterns, such as:

1. You delayed in seeking initial care;

2. Your symptoms appeared days or weeks after the traumatic event; and

3. You have gaps of time or delay when following through with treatment recommendations.

Any of the above arguments can be potentially successful in disrupting the chain of evidence that links the negligent event with the resulting trauma. Let's take a look at each of these arguments in further detail to understand how an insurer spins your healthcare records.

A. Delay in Seeking Initial Care

It is not uncommon for those in a motor vehicle collision to have mild or even no symptoms at the crash scene. Within days, however, symptoms increase and worsen. Some people will seek treatment right away, but others will take a wait-and-see approach. Many individuals feel that they can treat themselves with rest, heat, ice, or over-the-counter medication until the symptoms resolve. Some people will give this approach several days to work and some may wait several weeks or longer.

> *The longer the time period between the collision and documentation of the injury, the more likely the insurance company will state that there was an intervening cause of the injured party's condition.*

Also, a motor vehicle collision comes with phones calls, dreaded paperwork, and an uncertainty about insurance coverage. Waiting to learn what bills are covered or not often impacts a person's decision to seek healthcare.

Whatever the reason for the delay in seeking care, the insurance company will scrutinize the length of time that passes from the collision to the start of medical care. Since the condition claimed must be related in "direct sequence" to the collision, the longer the time period between the collision and documentation of the injury, the more likely the insurance company will state that there was an intervening cause of the injured party's condition.

B. Delay in the Onset of Symptoms

It is also common for a person involved in a traumatic event to feel fine at the scene but then develop symptoms over the next several hours to several days. Despite considerable medical literature explaining that the inflammatory process (read: pain) may take hours or days to take place, insurance companies attempt to deny responsibility for trauma-related injuries when the victim does not report immediate symptoms or pain.

The longer the time frame between the trauma and first treatment, the more aggressively the insurer will argue that the condition is not related to the traumatic event.

C. Delays When Following Through with the Treatment Plan

Even when an initial injury is documented close in time to the traumatic event, an injured person's lack of follow-through with the treatment recommended by his/her healthcare provider opens the door for the insurer to raise additional defenses.

First, if there is a gap in care because the patient has not followed through with the treatment recommendations, then the insurance company will argue that the initial trauma-related condition must have resolved, because truly injured people continue to seek treatment.

In other words, they suggest (often without any proof) that the injured party could have been newly injured from a new cause and that a return to treatment was the result of a new injury unrelated to the at-fault party's liability.

Gaps in treatment also give the insurer an opportunity to claim that the injured party did not comply with his or her doctor's treatment recommendations and, if he/she had, the condition would have resolved sooner. Just as an injured party has rights to be returned to pre-injury condition, he/she also has responsibilities to get well, otherwise known as *mitigation of damages*.

Mitigation of damages means that the injured person must take reasonable steps to lessen or reduce their own damages or injuries, such as seeking treatment and keeping the injury-related condition from worsening. The injured person must also follow through with the care that has been recommended by the treating healthcare provider.

If it can be shown that an injured person did not follow the treatment recommendations made by his or her healthcare provider, and if the insurance company can show that the lack of follow-through ultimately led to a worsening of injuries or a more prolonged and costly rehabilitation, then the insurer will likely succeed in its position that additional treatment costs are not reimbursable, since they were incurred as a result of the injured party's failure to obtain timely treatment.

The duty to mitigate is not absolute. Rather, it consists of what is "reasonable under the circumstances to avoid or minimize the damages."[1] Circumstances to be considered include lack of financial resources or insurance coverage to pay for treatment, transportation difficulties, or time management problems (for example, time constraints for single parents). The law also assumes that the injured party is an informed consumer and that he/she has a say in determining whether to continue care and the costs associated with that care.

There are several things an injury victim can do to minimize or eliminate the insurer's ability to make arguments based on delay in seeking initial care, delays in the onset of symptoms, and gaps in healthcare treatment follow-through.

a. Seek medical evaluation for any symptoms immediately after a traumatic event.

b. Report new symptoms to the healthcare provider promptly.

c. If seeking treatment several days after onset of pain, make clear to the healthcare provider when the symptoms actually began and why the delay in seeking care occurred. Having this noted helps to head off the insurance company's attempted denial.

d. If care has been established but you have not complied with treatment recommendations, explain to your healthcare provider the reason for the delay or failure to comply.

e. If an appointment must be missed, call ahead to cancel. A pattern of notations in the healthcare provider's chart of "No Show" or "Missed" can allow the insurance company to label you as irresponsible in your treatment follow-through and as having failed to mitigate your injuries and damages.

f. If an appointment with a healthcare provider is missed, report the reason to the healthcare provider and ask him/her to record the reason in the chart.

g. If a healthcare provider makes a recommendation that you know will be difficult to carry out, simply advise the healthcare provider of this issue and discuss alternatives.

---

1   *Sutton v. Shufelberger*, 31 Wn.App. 579, 643 P.2d 920 (1982)

Inside the Mind of a Former Insurance Attorney

A special thank you to Arthur D. Leritz, my colleague and attorney at Adler Giersch PS, for agreeing to write this section.

Mr. Leritz is no longer practicing law on behalf of insurance companies, but has left the "dark side of the force" and joined Adler Giersch PS in its representation of those with traumatic injuries. I am grateful that Mr. Leritz has willingly agreed to share the trade secrets of insurance attorneys. Arthur D. Leritz received his degree in Political Science from the University of Washington in 1996, followed by his Doctor of Jurisprudence from Willamette University College of Law in 1999.

Arthur D. Leritz:

Having recently ended an eleven year tenure as an insurance defense attorney, I can now share how I identified potential weaknesses in an injured party's case by noting mistakes that he or she would unwittingly make during treatment.

Now that I have left the "dark side," and started with Adler Giersch PS (a law firm that is highly respected by insurance adjusters and their attorneys) I want to share these secrets with you so that you will be better prepared, if and when you find yourself in this situation. These topics are in no specific order as any one of them can turn your case from a good one into one that could be coded "SIU"[1] by the insurance company, thereby making a case more difficult to settle.

---

1   "SIU" stands for Special Investigations Unit. It is a special section within an insurance company's organization that handles cases with elements of fraud. Any one of these subtopics within this chapter could put your case into SIU.

Not Following the Treatment Plan

It seems obvious, doesn't it? If your doctor recommends a specific course of treatment, then follow it. I used to often read through medical records and see recommendations made by healthcare providers that were not followed by the patient. For example, things like "patient referred for MRI two months ago, has yet to set appointment" or my absolute favorite: "patient is not complying with treatment recommendations." Upon seeing this, the insurance defense attorney is now free to argue that you must have healed from your injuries and any treatment after the date of the chart note is not necessary. Alternatively, it will be argued that if you had complied with treatment recommendations you would have been done treating sooner and your injuries, if any, would have resolved sooner. These are all ways to reduce the reasonableness of the compensation claim.

Doctor shopping raises several red flags to the insurance company.

Failing to show for evaluation and/or treatment appointments is also a big cause for concern from the insurance attorney's point of view. The phrase in a medical record that "Patient failed to show for appointment, failed to reschedule" gives the insurance attorney the same arguments as if you did not comply with the treatment recommendation. So, make sure you carefully follow your doctor's treatment recommendations; and if you do miss an appointment, make sure you explain to the provider why you missed the appointment and immediately reschedule.

Accurately Report Your Injuries

Getting involved in an automobile collision can be a very traumatic experience. All of a sudden, you will have to deal with doctors, insurance companies, bills and more correspondence than you are used to. In addition, patients can feel rushed, especially in an Emergency Room setting, with doctor appointments, but it remains very important to accurately report to your healthcare provider all of your injuries, even if some of your symptoms seem minor in comparison.

For example, I once had a case involving an injured motorcycle rider. He had a neck, mid back, and a right shoulder strain/sprain. He also had a sore ankle, but apparently figured that it would resolve on its own. So, he did not report the ankle problem to any of his medical providers. Unfortunately for the motorcycle rider, his ankle did not resolve on its own. In fact, the other injuries resolved 2-3 months later, but the ankle turned into a persistent problem. The first time he mentioned the ankle problem to his doctor was four months after the collision. Eventually, the ankle became such a problem that he needed surgery. The main defense to this ankle injury case was that the motorcycle rider did not sustain the ankle injury in the collision – otherwise he would have reported it to the ER doctor immediately after the traumatic incident and then his subsequent medical providers. At the deposition of his primary care provider, even his own doctor could not relate the ankle injury to the motorcycle collision, because of the gap of time from the collision to the first time the ankle injury showed up in the records. As a result, the motorcycle rider's attorney was unable to pursue that part of his claim and all medical bills relating to that ankle injury were not recovered.

Unfortunately for the motorcycle rider, since he downplayed his symptoms and did not report it, it looked to the insurance company that the ankle was not injured in the collision. The lesson here is simple: be accurate and thorough in reporting all your injuries, major and minor.

Doctor Shopping

I would occasionally get referred a case from an insurance adjuster, where the injured party sought treatment from numerous doctors in the first 6-12 months of a collision.

The injured party generally did not follow treatment recommendations by the same doctor, but instead went to a new doctor every time.

This is referred to as "doctor shopping," and it is interpreted by the insurer, as an injured party looking for a doctor that is going to tell them what they want to hear in terms of medications to prescribe or treatment they want to have. Doctor shopping raises several red flags to the insurance company.

First, it tells the insurance company that you are unwilling to follow doctor's recommendations. The natural conclusion from that is if you had done what you were told, your symptoms would have resolved sooner. Second, it allows the insurance company's attorney to argue that the injured party is a "flake" and is really not motivated to get better. Finally, this behavior creates fertile ground to argue that the patient is engaging in another behavior – drug seeking. Drug seeking behavior occurs when an injured person goes from doctor to doctor seeking pain medication to relieve their symptoms. In the realm of red flags, this is one of the big ones. It automatically tells the insurance company that you and your case are suspect. SIU, here you come.

Exaggerating the Facts

One of the worst things you can do to your personal injury case is try to make the injuries from trauma seem worse than they really are.

Rest assured that the insurance company and its attorneys are closely watching for this behavior in your records and will use every inconsistency in your medical records against you to attack your credibility.

My most notable example of exaggerating facts came a few years ago. It was a case involving a rear-end collision. After the incident, the injured party reported to the emergency room doctor that the collision occurred at around 5 miles per hour. A week later upon first seeing his primary care doctor after the rear-end collision, he reported it as a 10-12 miles per hour. After starting treatment with a chiropractor, the speed of the other driver had jumped to 15-20 miles per hour.

Such exaggeration undermines your credibility and allows the insurer to be suspicious about all that you do and say. It may also allow them to argue that you are actively trying to manipulate the facts to engineer a better case. So, be accurate *and* consistent in relating the facts to your care providers.

Perceived Inability to Pay for Treatment

The inability of injured parties to pay for necessary medical treatment after a collision certainly adds insult to injury. But it remains critical for you to attend to your medical needs. You cannot simply say that you have no PIP or health insurance, when in fact you may have benefits available. But before you think you cannot pay for treatment, it is important to consider what options you may have available and that you explored all avenues of payment before giving up.

The worst thing you can do in this situation is not get the treatment you need because you cannot pay for it. As harsh as it may seem, the insurance company will use this against you by claiming that you are not trying hard enough to fulfill your duty to get well.

I have taken many depositions over the years and it amazed me when someone would claim they did not treat because they had no insurance; even when they had coverage but did not know about it! Be prepared and do not hesitate to ask the insurance company and your providers about options concerning payment. There generally is a way to make this happen, if you pursue all the options. Certainly, your attorney representing you should be able to explain and explore all the options.

Getting Back to Activities Too Prematurely

Your main priority when recovering from trauma is to get well. There seems to be a tendency however, especially in men, to try to get back to prior activities too prematurely. And this can backfire and undermine your claim. For example, I had a case where a construction worker was involved in a motor vehicle collision and hit his knee on the dash of his truck. He had some inflammation and soreness with his knee, but it was never properly diagnosed. After he returned to work, he re-injured the same knee. The insurance adjuster picked up on this and claimed that the knee injury

There seems to be a tendency however, especially in men, to try to get back to prior activities too prematurely. And this can backfire and undermine your claim.

was related to a work incident and not the motor vehicle collision. He should have had his doctor clear him to return to work after the collision, and before returning to work. His decision to return to work prematurely resulted in muddied waters on whether his knee pain was from the collision v. work injury.

Telling the Truth

When it comes to medical history, I used to see many cases where the injured party had what I would politely call "memory loss." If you fill out the form at your doctor's office and write "none" under prior collisions or previous injuries to the same area, that used to be the first thing I would highlight in records and then, the hunt was on. I would search for other medical records and when I found old records that directly contradicted the statements made in the records after the collision, then the compensation value of the case would decreased by at least 30%. This does not undermine the severity of the injuries from the collision, but it opened the door to undermine the credibility of the injured party with inconsistent statements. I agree that this may seem a bit harsh, but the insurer will want its attorneys to argue anything and everything that can decrease the value of a case during settlement discussions or in the eyes of jurors.

Social Media - A Blessing and a Curse

Networking sites like Facebook and MySpace help folks to connect with friends and family. These are fantastic resources, but remember that everything you say on these sites and every picture you post or comment on can be accessed, even if you think your user preferences are keeping such information private. Remember, there is no privacy on the internet.

> *Everything you say on these sites and every picture you post or comment on can be accessed, even if you think your user preferences are keeping such information private. Remember, there is no privacy on the internet.*

Searching these and other social networking sites are chock full of statements and pictures of those with traumatic injuries. The stuff people say when they think no one is looking still amazes me.

I had a case once involving a particularly bad wrist injury from a trip and fall. The injured woman had to have several surgeries and had quite a bit of functional limitations and pain, despite the best medical efforts. I checked her Facebook page the night before her deposition and found that in the previous several weeks she was talking about having gone motorcycle riding and had several photos of herself in various places waving to the camera, with the injured wrist mind you. She was even talking to friends about what she was going to do once she settled her case and what to say at her deposition. Needless to say, it was a very uncomfortable deposition for her. And her attorney was not pleased or aware of what his client was saying on the internet.

I had another case involving a young woman who was involved in a rear-end collision and was claiming some pretty substantial and permanent injuries. By the time I got the file from the insurance company, it already had several pages of the young woman's Facebook page printed out, talking about how tired she was from playing tennis, and how mean her aerobics instructor was and how hard those hour long workouts were.

Mitigating Damages

When you have a traumatic injury, the law provides you with the right for compensation for your losses. With that comes a duty to mitigate your damages. This means that you have to take advantage of every opportunity to reduce your economic and physical losses. As a result, it is important to follow your treatment plan, and return to work when you are medically released to do so.

If you do not mitigate your damages then a good defense attorney will use it against you and argue that if you had followed your treatment plan, or had gone back to work when told to, then your economic damages would be less than the amount claimed.

Failing to mitigate can also have a big impact on your credibility with a jury, so be very mindful of this and take every reasonable effort to mitigate your damages.

PRE-EXISTING CONDITIONS

CHAPTER 25

A classic and often-used argument made by an insurer to deny all or part of a personal injury claim is that the traumatic injury is related to a pre-existing condition.

Under the law there are only two types of pre-existing conditions. The first is known as an "inactive" or "dormant" pre-existing condition. The second is known as an "active" or "symptomatic" pre-existing condition. The difference between an active and inactive pre-existing condition in a medical-legal-insurance context is significant, and can make all the difference in the outcome of a personal injury claim.

An *inactive* pre-existing condition is one in which, at the time of the traumatic injury, there were no symptoms or treatment related to that prior condition. An *active* pre-existing condition is one that predated the traumatic injury and was causing symptoms.

A. Inactive Pre-Existing Condition

Washington law states that if there is no evidence that a pre-existing condition caused pain or disability before trauma is sustained, then the "lighting up" of that pre-existing condition makes the at-fault party liable for all damages caused to the injured person. With inactive pre-existing condition, there is no prior pain or disability to differentiate from the injuries caused by the new trauma.

From the medical-legal perspective, the proximate cause of the reason for the present symptoms is the recent injury, although the symptoms may be worse or healing may take longer because of the pre-existing condition.

Washington courts have addressed this issue many times. For example, the 1969 Supreme Court addressed the issue in *Bennett v. Messick.*[1] In that case, the injured party was employed as a fruit picker who was injured when he was hit by a forklift. There were several injuries, including an injury to the same ankle that he had injured 40 years earlier while playing basketball. The evidence showed that the prior injury had healed normally and that the injured party suffered no pain or residuals in the ankle thereafter, until the tractor accident. Testimony indicated, however, that a degenerative arthritic process was present in the left ankle, presumably caused by the basketball injury 40 years earlier. The treating doctor testified that the forklift injury caused pain and limitation of motion within the ankle because it aggravated the "asymptomatic" arthritic condition. He further testified that without the tractor injury superimposed on the earlier injury, the chances were better than 50/50 that the injured party would never have had a medical problem with the ankle. The court reaffirmed the applicable rule in this area, by stating:

> The rule is that when a latent condition itself does not cause pain, suffering, or a disability, but that condition plus an injury brings on pain or disability by aggravating the preexisting condition and making it active, then the injury, and not the dormant condition, is the proximate cause of the pain and disability. Thus, the party at fault is held for the entire damages as a result of the accident.

More recently, the Washington Supreme Court decided *Harris v. Drake*[2] (2004) which reaffirmed the law stated in *Bennett v. Messick.* In the *Harris* case the court learned that Bradley Harris, a painter, was injured in a motor vehicle collision by Doris Drake. Mr. Harris suffered back and shoulder injuries that ultimately resulted in arthroscopic shoulder surgery. When attempts by Harris's attorney to settle the matter failed, a lawsuit was filed and Ms. Drake's insurance company hired an attorney for her. Ms. Drake's attorney claimed that Mr. Harris' shoulder injury was related to a "pre-existing condition," not the car collision because:

a. An MRI performed one month after the motor vehicle collision showed a normal shoulder;

---

1   76 Wn. 2d 474 (1969)
2   152 Wn. 2d. 480 (2004)

b. Mr. Harris's shoulder problem appeared only after he was released by his doctor to resume his painting job; and

c. Mr. Harris's own surgeon testified that painters often have impingement syndrome problems caused by their profession.

Despite the insurance company attorney's argument, there was no evidence at trial that Mr. Harris had a shoulder problem prior to the motor vehicle collision. The jury sided with Mr. Harris. Ms. Drake's attorney appealed the case.

The Supreme Court in *Harris v. Drake* reaffirmed the precedent in *Bennett v. Messick* when ruling:

> Even allowing for the possibility of a preexisting condition, the defense failed to show that such condition was symptomatic prior to the accident. When an accident lights up and makes active a preexisting condition that was dormant and asymptomatic immediately prior to the accident, the preexisting condition is not a proximate cause of the resulting damages.

When a prior injury or condition is present, effective communication between you and your treating doctor is vital. You must be clear with the provider about prior conditions. If the prior condition was fully resolved and was not causing any symptoms prior to the traumatic injury, you should say so. You should also be clear about your activity level prior to the accident and the changes in activities following the accident. Otherwise, your doctor may assume that since you had neck or back pain previously that your current neck and back condition is somehow related to that.

Even when the injury victim has no history of a prior injury or condition, insurers and medical examiners often attempt to link prior conditions to the cause of post-trauma symptoms. Most often this occurs when interpreting X-rays or an MRI report following a traumatic event. These films often reveal "degenerative" changes (wear and tear) of a joint or in the spine. It is quite common, particularly as people age, to have degenerative changes that do not cause symptoms or pain at all. However, since these conditions can cause symptoms and may make a joint more susceptible to injury, the insurer may argue that the pre-existing degeneration, or age in general, is the full

RICHARD H. ADLER
Attorney at Law, Adler Giersch PS

or partial cause of the injured person's post-trauma symptoms and ongoing residual pain.

A medical research study published in *Spine*, "A Cross-Sectional Study Correlating Degeneration of the Cervical Spine and Disability and Pain in United Kingdom Patients," refutes the insurer's argument. This study, as described by the authors, ". . . was designed to investigate the relation between degenerative changes in all joints of the cervical spine as well as pain and disability. The link between pain and disability levels and impending litigation was also studied."[3]

In the study, X-rays and questionnaire data from 180 consecutive patients with neck pain were collected. The questionnaires asked each patient how chronic their problems were, the cause of their pain, and whether their injuries involved an associated pending legal action. The X-rays were evaluated for degenerative changes.

The authors found no statistically significant differences in pain severity or disability levels between the patients with and without cervical degeneration. Additionally, according to the findings, the location and severity of degeneration in the discs and spinal joints were not related to the levels of pain and disability.

The authors summarize and discuss their study by stating:

> Patients with neck pain resulting from trauma report significantly more pain and disability than patients with neck pain who have no trauma history. However, trauma patients do not have more degeneration in their cervical spines. Because so few patients in this study were involved in litigation related to the trauma episodes, impending litigation was not a factor in the higher pain and disability levels. The increased symptoms most likely reflect soft-tissue injury. *The presence of degenerative changes in the cervical spine of trauma patients should not be regarded as causing or contributing to the levels of pain and disability reported* (emphasis added).

---

3   Peterson, et al, *Spine* 2003. Volume 28 pages 129-133

B. Active Pre-Existing Condition

Let's now take a look at the second type of pre-existing condition. When you have a pre-existing condition that was causing pain or requiring some level of healthcare at the time of the recent traumatic injury, this is known as an *active* or symptomatic preexisting condition. In this situation, the patient's treating doctor will be asked to provide an opinion that splits the cause of the current condition into old and new – this is called the *apportionment* opinion.

> *The patient's treating doctor will be asked to provide an opinion that splits the cause of the current condition into old and new – this is called the apportionment opinion.*

The doctor will base his/her apportionment opinion on a number of factors, including the patient's report of pre- and post-collision pain levels and restrictions, the patient's prior records, objective tests and other factors. Essentially, the doctor will indicate a percentage of the condition that is related to the preexisting condition and to the recent traumatic injury.

When there is an active pre-existing condition, the law allows the injured party to recover only the percentage of damages that are related to the traumatic injury.

For example, consider the case of a person who had an active pre-existing back injury that was worsened by a car collision. The doctor's opinion is that only 30 percent of the post-collision condition is related to the traumatic event and 70 percent predates the trauma. The injury in question, if not for the prior condition, had a value of $50,000. In this situation, the injured person will receive only 30 percent of the $50,000, or $15,000. As you can see, the responsible insurance company will be fighting hard to make the pre-existing percentage as high as possible, as it reduces the amount they have to pay.

ACCUSING YOU OF
FAKING YOUR INJURIES

CHAPTER 26

When the facts and law of a case do not favor the insurance company, they resort to accusing the injured person of faking their injuries or playing the system in order to get a higher level of compensation.

This innuendo is intended to raise suspicion against the credibility of the injured party. Here are a few arguments to anticipate.

A. The Secondary Gain Argument

The "secondary gain" argument made by insurance companies goes like this: the patient is motivated to get treatment in order to get a bigger settlement. If it weren't for the prospect of winning a personal injury claim, this person would have been fine long ago.

Being hurt is working for them – they think it will get them more money. In other words, many insurers argue that an injured person is simply trying to bilk the system for their own monetary gain.

A study published in the June 26, 2001 issue of *Neurology,* the scientific journal of the American Academy of Neurology, refutes this claim. The study titled "Handicap After Acute Whiplash Injury, a 1-year Prospective Study of Risk Factors," states that *"initiation of [a] lawsuit within [the] first month after injury did not influence recovery."*

This study examined 141 Danish patients who were involved in rear-end car collisions. All patients had gone to the emergency room with complaints of neck pain or headaches within two days of their accidents.

Risk factors such as patients' previous head injuries, severe initial head-aches, neck pain intensity, and range of motion were found to be the best predictors of long-term handicap after a whiplash injury and that having a claim was not related to the length of care or recovery.

B. Litigation Neurosis

Similar to the "secondary gain" argument, insurers often claim that personal injury claims or lawsuits are the result of "litigation neurosis."

The term litigation neurosis became popular following a 1961 study by Dr. Henry Miller, a prominent British neurologist. He reported on two hundred head injury patients with long-term subjective complaints whose cases were still under insurance review. Based on his conclusion that 24 percent of his patients with worker's compensation and personal injury claims were suffering from psychoneurotic complaints with no organic basis, insurers have subsequently labeled many patients as neurotic in one form or another. In Miller's view, only persons with the opportunity for compensation developed post-concussion syndrome. All but four of the forty-five cases returned to work after their claims were settled. Therefore, Miller concluded that settlement of the claim helped them return to work.[1]

Miller's work has received growing criticism over the years. Never-theless, his article remains influential in medical-legal circles today, predominantly used as leverage by insurers and insurance defense attorneys who argue that patients claiming post-concussive syndrome or residuals from soft tissue injury suffer from a functional (psycho-logical) rather than an objective physical basis.

Here is how this argument is used: Cervical spine and concussion-type injuries are a common result of motor vehicle collisions. Injured persons often present symptoms such as forgetfulness, irritability, cognitive deficits, sleeping difficulties, headaches, visual disturbances, and neck pain. Some physicians may be hard-pressed to account for these symptoms on a physical basis, since some are subjective in nature: no test can prove the existence of symptoms such as headache or forgetfulness. In some cases, the doctors hired by the insurance

---

1   *See British Medical Journal, 1961, Vol. 1, pp. 919-925 and 992-998*

company to conduct IMEs (see Chapter 21 of this book) label the injured party with "litigation neurosis" when a MRI or CT scan fails to produce objective evidence of injury.

Recent research, however, has provided compelling evidence that such subjective complaints arise from organic and objective injuries, despite being hard to see on common imaging tests such as x-ray, MRI, or CT Scan.

A research article by Arthur Croft, Doctor of Chiropractic (DC) in the *Journal of Neuromusculoskeletal System,* provided an exhaustive review of all literature concerning "litigation neurosis." Dr. Croft's review of the published research studies provides compelling evidence that the terms "litigation neurosis" or "compensation neurosis" should be abandoned. According to Dr. Croft, the literature indicates:

* In 1965, dePalma and Subin reported that only 25 percent of three hundred eighty six of their patients became involved in litigation and the treatment outcome was no different in the litigation and non-litigation groups.

* In 1968, Schutt and Dohanv published their analysis of women injured in whiplash type accidents and reported no significant difference in the prevalence of symptoms in patients with pending litigation versus those whose litigation had been resolved.

* Hohl, in 1974, found that in litigated cases, those whose claims were settled after eighteen months had a worse prognosis than those settling in the first six months. Predictably, prolonged treatment will be correlated with protracted litigation and a worse prognosis. However, of the non-litigated group, only 50 percent were found to be asymptomatic at a five-year follow-up period.

* In 1988, Maimaris et al., published the results of their retro-spective study of 102 whiplash patients and concluded that liti-gation did not influence the natural progression of symptoms since all litigating patients were symptomatic for two to two and one half years following injury, even though the average time until settlement was nine months.

✳ Hodgson and Grundy, in 1989, reported on a group of forty patients who had been injured in a whiplash trauma (twenty six had been exposed to rear impact trauma). The follow-up period varied from ten to fifteen years. The thirty patients who remained unchanged since settlement provided more evidence that resolution of symptoms does not always follow settlement of legal claims.

✳ In 1991, Watkinson et al., evaluated a group of individuals suffering from cervical acceleration/deceleration soft tissue injuries. They found that 86 percent were continuing to complain of symptoms after a mean follow-up period of 10.8 years. The study argued that the increased symptomatic degenerative changes noted on cervical spine X-rays after ten years refutes the notion of compensation neurosis and argues for an organic lesion.

✳ Pennie and Agambar in 1991 reported that no statistically significant correlation existed between the recovery of litigated and non-litigated cases of cervical acceleration/deceleration injuries. This finding is echoed by Parmar and Raymakers (1993), who wrote that their group of one hundred patients was followed for a mean of eight years after injury. The majority of their cases were free of significant pain before the settlement of their claims, and only four improved soon after settlement.

✳ In 1993, Robinson and Cassar-Pullicino published that the majority of their cases (86 percent) ranging from ten to nineteen years after injury remained symptomatic after settlement.

Understanding how and why insurers use and misuse labels such as "secondary gain," "faker," and "litigations neurosis" is an important element in preventing them from wrongfully denying legitimate claims for physical, economic, and emotional recovery.

THE DARK SIDE OF INSURANCE

For those readers that want to dig deeper into understanding how our insurance system is supposed to work to protect policyholders, and how the traditional rules of insurance are not followed by the insurers (such as Allstate), there is a truly remarkable book written by attorney David H. Berardinelli, published in 2008, called *From Good Hands to Boxing Gloves: The Dark Side of Insurance.*

As noted in Mr. Berardinelli's book, our insurance system is founded on two key rules: the *indemnity principle* and the *fiduciary principle*. Together these principles are intended to level the playing field between the insurance company and you, the policyholder. In short, these principles balance the insurer's legitimate goal of being profitable while allowing you, as the insured policyholder, to get prompt and fair payment for covered losses.

Verity Jane Smith/Photodisc/PunchStock

Berardinelli explains in more detail:

> Casualty insurance is a unique insurance product. It's different from other kinds of insurance like life insurance. Life insurance pays a set benefit when you die regardless of the cause or consequences of your death.

Casualty insurance is *indemnity* coverage. It doesn't pay a set benefit. It pays as much as the policyholder needs, up to the policy's limit, "to restore an insured to the same financial position after the loss that he or she was in prior to the loss." In the language of insurance, to *indemnify* someone means to make them whole again. That means the insured doesn't get paid more than the actual loss. It also means the insured shouldn't get paid less than what it takes to make the insured whole again. The insurer's duty to pay the *full* amount the insured needs to be put back in the same position he or she was in before the loss is the *indemnity principle*.

> An insurer violates the indemnity principle by paying less than the full value of the loss. That doesn't make the insured whole. It leaves the insured worse off financially. You pay the insurance company to assume the financial burden of the loss.

If you still have to pay for part of the loss yourself, you're worse off. Your standard of living goes down because you have to borrow, take from savings, or do without, until you can afford to replace the loss. When that happens, you don't get the benefits you paid for when you bought insurance. The *fiduciary principle* was also developed to balance the relationship between insurer and policyholder. This principle is based on the idea that insurers act like banks. Like banks, insurers are entrusted with the public's money (premiums) which they promise to pay when the public needs it. This idea — that insurers act like banks — has been around for a very long time in insurance law. As the United State Supreme Court stated in 1914:

> The contracts of insurance may be said to be interdependent. They cannot be regarded singly, or isolatedly, and *the effect of their relation is to create a fund of assurance and credit, the companies becoming the depositories of the money of the insured,* possessing great power thereby, and charged with great responsibility . . . On the other hand, to the insured, insurance is an asset, a basis of credit . . . It is, therefore, essentially different from

ordinary commercial transactions, and . . . is of the greatest public concern (emphasis added).

Like banks, insurers accept their policyholders' money and keep it for them, promising to pay the full amount of their policyholders' covered losses. Promising to keep somebody else's money until they need it demands a high standard of conduct on the part of the person holding the money.

Banks can't tell you it's too much trouble for them to honor your withdrawal slip, or ask you to withdraw less than you need. In the same way, insurance companies shouldn't intentionally delay your claim or ask you to accept less than your claim is worth.

Making a claim is the same as withdrawing money from a joint bank account. That account has your name and thousands of other account owner's names. You can't withdraw all the money in the account, because not all the money belongs to you. You have to prove to the teller who you are and that your name is on the account. That's like providing the insurer with proof that you're covered under the policy for a loss you have suffered.

Most important, the bank can't treat the money in this joint account as its own. The joint account holders own the money, not the bank. The bank can invest or loan the money while it's in the account — that's how the bank makes money. However, the bank can't just dip into this joint account whenever it wants to boost its profits, or pay its shareholders extra dividends, or pay its executives large bonuses. That would be like embezzling from the account owners.

Like a bank, the insurer must be helpful and assist its policyholders to withdraw their fair share from the claims account as promptly as possible. The insurer can't deliberately make it harder than it needs to be for the policyholders to get the full amount they need to put them back to where they were before the loss.

The insurer can't deliberately delay paying legitimate claims by asking for useless information or demanding more proof than it really needs. It can't delay payment or force policyholders to jump through needless hoops, in hopes they'll give up or take less than the full and fair amount of the benefits they're owed under the policy.

The insurer can't pressure policyholders who are in a financial bind into accepting a quick payment that's far less than what they need to make them whole. It can't deliberately force policy-holders to file needless, expensive, and time consuming lawsuits as the only way to get what they need to fully restore them to where they were before the loss.

Together, the indemnity principle and the fiduciary principle encompass the traditional insurance laws and rules that govern how insurers are supposed to treat their policyholders. They also govern how the casualty insurance industry is supposed to operate. Under these traditional rules, insurers owe special duties to policyholder to pay their legitimate claims fairly (the indemnity principle) *and* promptly (the fiduciary principle).

It is when insurers put their own financial interests ahead of their insured's needs that the system is no longer fair. The playing field is no longer level, and an insured either accepts less than they deserve or seeks legal counsel to level the field.

RICHARD H. ADLER
Attorney at Law, Adler Giersch PS

Insurance Commissioner: Complaint Process

CHAPTER 28

We previously discussed some remedies that you have when your auto insurer delays payment of your claim or refuses to pay, at pages 25–30 including a discussion on Hiring an Attorney to Handle Your Trauma Injury Case at pages 114–126). There is another option available to you through Washington's Insurance Commissioner.

The Washington State Office of the Insurance Commissioner has many roles, including assisting consumers with insurance complaints and inquires. They have the authority to investigate complaints against insurers and agents, assist in providing dispute resolution, and enforce insurance law on behalf of consumers. Here is what the Insurance Commissioner's office can and cannot do.

Can:

1. Present your complaint to the insurance company.

2. Obtain information or explanations on your behalf from the insurance company or its representatives. This may involve written and verbal contact with the companies or persons.

> The Washington State Office of the Insurance Commissioner has many roles, including assisting consumers with insurance complaints and inquires. They have the authority to investigate complaints against insurers and agents.

3. Review in detail the information received from the company and compliance with applicable laws, regulations, and policy contracts.

4. Serve as an advocate to help resolve your insurance concerns.

5. Explain what your insurance policy covers.

6. Suggest actions or procedures you may take that could aid in resolving your insurance problem.

Cannot:

1. Act as your lawyer or give you legal advice.

2. Recommend or give an opinion on an insurance company, agent, or policy.

3. Identify an insurance company with whom a particular person or entity may have a policy.

4. Resolve disputes of fact between you and the insurance company. For example:

   a. Who is negligent or at fault;

   b. Who might be telling the truth in the matter when accounts of the matter differ; or

   c. The value of a claim or the amount of money owed to you.

5. Make medical judgment.

6. Force a company to satisfy you if no laws have been broken – even if you believe the company or agent has been unfair, unreasonable, or deceitful.

7. Handle problems with your employer's self-funded health plan, unless the plan involves an insurance company or HMO licensed in the State of Washington.

RICHARD H. ADLER
Attorney at Law, Adler Giersch PS

Though the Insurance Commissioner's office can be helpful on occasion, it does not have authority or jurisdiction of all areas of insurance. Specifically, they do not have the ability to assist with:

1. Worker's Compensation claims (for information, contact Washington State Department of Labor & Industries).

2. Third-party administrators or provider networks.

3. Federal employees' health and life insurance (contact Office of Personnel Management).

4. Military insurance (contact Tricare).

5. Policies purchased in another state (contact the state of purchase).

6. Basic Health Plan (contact Washington State Health Care Authority).

7. Uniform Medical Plan (contact Washington State Health Care Authority).

A. Filing a Complaint Against an Insurance Company

To file a complaint with the Insurance Commissioner, complete the form on the following pages and mail it to the Insurance Commissioner's Office at PO Box 40256, Olympia, WA 98506. Or you can also complete the form electronically on the Commission's website: www.insurance.wa.gov/consumers.complaint.asp.

Here are tips to make sure the Commissioner's investigators have the information they need to handle your case:

1. *Print* all names, addresses, and phone contact numbers.

2. Make sure to *list name and address* of person insured if it is different from the individual completing the form.

3. Include the *type of policy* involved, as well as *the claim number* and *the policy number*.

4. If your complaint involves a claim, list the *date of loss*. This is the day on which the accident or situation occurred, leading to the loss that is involved in this complaint.

5. Don't forget to include the *name of the insurance company*, as well as the company's address and phone number, and the agent's name and address, if you are dealing with your own company on a claim. If you are dealing with another company's insurance coverage, list the company's name, address, and phone number, the name and phone number of the adjuster handling the claim, and the claim number (if you know it).

6. Check the box next to the explanation that best describes your complaint. If none of the listed explanation fit your situation, check "Other" and then briefly list another explanation in your own words. Use the second side of the form and additional paper, if necessary, to explain in more detail what happened to you, the order of events, and why you believe the problem occurred. Only send paper photocopied documents (be sure to keep your originals). Do not send video or audio materials.

7. At the bottom of the form, list the things that you feel must happen in order to resolve your complaint to your satisfaction.

For more information or any questions concerning complaints, simply call the commissioner's toll-free Insurance Commissioner Hotline at 1-800-562-6900.

B. How to File Your Complaint:
Complaints must be submitted:

1. Online at www.insurance.wa.gov/consumers/complaint.asp.

2. By fax: (360) 586-2018

3. By mail: PO Box 40256, Olympia, WA 988504-0256

   a. Include copies of documentation that support your complaint. Only send paper documents (be sure to keep your original documents). Do not send video or audio materials.

   b. Be specific, list each issue to be considered.

   c. *If the complaint involves medical issues, the patient's signature or the legal guardian's signature must appear on the authorization for release of medical information.*

C. How Long Does the Insurance Commissioner's Office Take to Investigate Your Complaint?

On average, it takes thirty days from the time a complaint is received until finalized. If your complaint involves a unique or complex problem, it may take longer.

D. What Results Can You Expect From the Insurance Commissioner's Office Investigation?

* If the Insurance Commissioner's Analyst is not satisfied with the company's response, he or she will continue to work on your file. This may involve additional letters and phone calls to the company.

* The Commissioner's Office should pursue every reasonable avenue available to them to assure a positive outcome for you.

* If they see no evidence of violations of law or rule, they will contact you explaining why they are closing the investigation.

* Your complaint will become a permanent part of the company's public record with the commissioner's office. This is very important, as further legal reforms on an insurer's conduct starts by tracking the volume and similarity of complaints.

Need more help? Call the Insurance Consumer Hotline 1-800-562.6900! The professional consumer advocates help enforce insurance law and can investigate complaints against insurance companies and agents on your behalf.

STATUTE OF LIMITATIONS
CHAPTER 29

A. What is it?

When you are injured by another, an invisible clock begins to tick. This clock is more formally known as the "Statute of Limitations."

Failure to settle a claim or bring a lawsuit within the time period set by law will extinguish the injured party's legal rights to recover for their injuries.

If the time period expires, a court will dismiss the case without consideration of the case's merits or the reasons for delay.

The traditional purposes of the Statute of Limitations rule were to bar claims for which "evidence has been lost, memories faded and witnesses disappeared," according to the 1944 case from the United States Supreme Court, *RR Telegraphers v. Railway Express.*[11] Other justifications for such a law include allowing individuals to dispose of old records after a certain length of time; creating closure and certainty by allowing individuals to get on with their lives without legal intrusions from the past; insuring that neither party is prejudiced by undue delay; and discouraging stale and fraudulent claims.

This area of law can be complex. For example, the length of time allowed to file a lawsuit may depend upon the state in which the injury

1   [1]321 US 342 (1944)

RICHARD H. ADLER
Attorney at Law, Adler Giersch PS

occurred; the type of negligence involved (automobile v. professional negligence)[2]; the age of the injured party (minor v. adult)[3]; when the injury was discovered; whether the injured party or the person causing the injury dies; and whether the lawsuit includes state law, federal law, or both. One thing is certain, there are different Statute of Limitations periods for virtually every cause of action and/or situation.

B. When the At-Fault Party is a City, County, State, or Federal Government

If the responsible party is a government entity or employee in the scope of his/her governmental duties, one must file an administrative claim for damages *before* a lawsuit may be started. This prerequisite step is quite tricky since it requires the injured party to also file a written claim with the proper governmental entity, using a proper form, and within a certain period of time or be forever barred from recovery.

C. Uninsured and Underinsured Motorist

In cases where the responsible party is either an uninsured motorist (UM) or underinsured motorist (UIM), the Statute of Limitations is not governed by state tort or personal injury law, but rather by the terms of the contract between an auto insurer and its insured.

Under current Washington laws, a UM or UIM claim is viewed as a contract action carrying a six-year Statute of Limitations, even though the underlying personal injury claim stems from a motor vehicle collision carrying a three-year time limit.

---

2   **Malpractice**: The Statute of Limitations for medical malpractice varies widely from state to state. In most states, the statutes of limitations clock does not begin to tick until the injured party becomes aware of his/her injury, as in a medical malpractice claim where the facts or the impact of the doctor's mistake are not immediately apparent. In Washington, the Statute of Limitations law provides that actions against health-care providers must be filed within three years of the date that the act giving rise to the injury occurred; *or* within one year after the date the injury was, or should have been, discovered, whichever is later. In no event may a medical malpractice action be filed more than eight years after the act giving rise to the injury.

3   **Adults**: In most states, the Statute of Limitations clock begins at the moment of the act causing the injury. **Minors**: In most states, including Washington, the Statute of Limitations clock starts to tick on a minor's 18th birthday.

D. State by State Automobile Negligence and Statutes of Limitations

The following state by state list shows Statute of Limitation laws that exist in the United States for automobile injury claims. Each state is free to set different time limits on different types of legal actions, such as professional negligence, real estate transactions, contract breaches, assaults, etc.

Caution: Do not rely upon this information for your own personal situation. Statutes frequently change or are modified by the state legislature, and different injury circumstances require other statutes and notice provisions to be applied. The law can get complicated in this area so it is recommended you seek competent legal advice from an attorney on your specific situation.

Alabama	2 yrs.	Kentucky	1 yr.	N. Dakota	6 yrs.
Alaska	2 yrs.	Louisiana	1 yr.	Ohio	2 yrs.
Arizona	2 yrs.	Maine	6 yrs.	Oklahoma	2 yrs.
Arkansas	5 yrs.	Maryland	3 yrs.	Oregon	2 yrs.
California	2 yrs.	Massachusetts	3 yrs.	Pennsylvania	2 yrs.
Colorado	2 yrs.	Michigan	3 yrs.	Rhode Island	3 yrs.
Connecticut	2 yrs.	Minnesota	2 yrs.	S. Carolina	3 yrs.
Delaware	2 yrs.	Mississippi	3 yrs.	S. Dakota	3 yrs.
DC	3 yrs.	Missouri	5 yrs.	Tennessee	1 yr.
Florida	4 yrs.	Montana	3 yrs.	Texas	2 yrs.
Georgia	2 yrs.	Nebraska	4 yrs.	Utah	4 yrs.
Hawaii	2 yrs.	Nevada	2 yrs.	Vermont	3 yrs.
Idaho	2 yrs.	New Hampshire	3 yrs.	Virginia	2 yrs.
Illinois	2 yrs.	New Jersey	2 yrs.	Washington	3 yrs.
Indiana	2 yrs.	New Mexico	3 yrs.	West Virginia	2 yrs.
Iowa	2 yrs.	New York	3 yrs.	Wisconsin	3 yrs.
Kansas	2 yrs.	N. Carolina	2 yrs.	Wyoming	4 yrs.

E. Children

The Statute of Limitations for children (defined as less than 18 years in Washington) is different than the one for adults (defined as 18 years or older).

In Washington, for those that are under 18 years, involved in a traumatic injury, and pursuing a personal injury claim, the Statute of Limitations clock starts ticking when they first reach their 18th birthday.

For example, an adult in a motor vehicle collision in Washington has three years from the date of the collision to settle their claim or decide to file a lawsuit. For a child, the three-year Statute of Limitations for injuries in a motor vehicle collision begins not at the time of the collision, but three years from his/her 18th birthday.

F. Word of Caution

This chapter is not intended as a guide for determining what Statute of Limitations applies in a particular case. Instead, it is to give the reader a general working knowledge of the complexities of how the Statute of Limitation laws operate. The most important thing to remember about Statute of Limitation laws is that failure to file a lawsuit before the expiration of the applicable limita-

Each state is free to set different time limits on different types of legal actions.

tions period will bar that claim, regardless of its merits. Given the complexities in this area of the law and the harsh consequence of barring an otherwise valid claim, one should use caution and seek legal advice early.

Hiring an Attorney to Handle Your Traumatic Injury Case

The medical-legal-insurance fields of traumatic injury are highly specialized. You want to make sure that the attorney you select is able to provide the legal representation and advocacy you need and deserve. An attorney should be contacted as soon as possible after the traumatic injury to ensure the information and evidence surrounding the injury is properly preserved.

A. Do I Need an Attorney?

Anxiety caused by a traumatic injury should not be unnecessarily compounded by worry about insurance claims. Whether to use the services of an attorney or negotiate a claim by yourself may seem like a simple decision. Most people believe that their insurance company or the other party's company will handle everything and that will be the end of it. And insurers now train their claim representatives to suggest that hiring an attorney involved will only result in 'giving away' one-third of what they were going to give you in the first place. Unfortunately, as we discussed in earlier chapters of this book, it's quite common for traumatically injured individuals to be misled or intimidated into forfeiting some or all of their legal rights by insurers.

> It's quite common for traumatically injured individuals to be misled or intimidated into forfeiting some or all of their legal rights.

Laws relating to personal injury and insurance are complex and subject to frequent change, as are the medical and scientific arenas of traumatic injury. The expertise of the properly selected attorney is invaluable not only in dealing with insurance matters on your behalf, but also in interpreting and explaining insurance contracts and the law. An attorney experienced in traumatic injury knows how to obtain fair and reasonable compensation for your injuries by gathering liability and medical evidence, and negotiating with insurance companies. A good attorney in this area of practice will also have familiarity with court procedures, filing requirements, deadlines, and other details could be easily overlooked by a non-lawyer.

An attorney with specific experience in the area of traumatic injury will have knowledge of the resources necessary to properly evaluate and present your case. These resources will include hiring expert witnesses, such as a private investigator, accident reconstructionist, neurologist, medical rehabilitation doctor, radiologist, psychiatrist, neuropsychologist, vocational rehabilitation counselor, physical capacities evaluator, economist, or a life-care planning specialist, among others.

Cases involving traumatic injury often involve several insurance companies, governmental programs, and disability insurers. An attorney will help coordinate benefits to ensure maximum compensation, protect your rights, and provide resources to assist you with these issues.

When you hire an attorney experienced in handling traumatic injury cases, all of the resources and support staff of a highly trained professional are on your side to protect your legal rights.

Traumatic injuries create physical limitations and financial stresses that can slow down the healing process. With the right attorney, the client/patient can focus on the main goal of healing and getting well.

B. Can I Afford an Attorney?

In personal injury cases, most attorneys work on a contingency fee basis. This means that the attorney agrees to provide the legal representation you need with payment for services occurring at the time of settlement or a verdict from the jury. Basically, the contingency fee arrangement allows the client the opportunity to hire the best attorney in the field, without paying an hourly fee or receiving monthly bills for legal services. Remember, the opposing insurance company will spend whatever it takes to try to disprove the extent of your injuries and minimize what they should pay. This means you need to obtain the best legal representation possible. Typically a contingency fee will amount to one-third of the final settlement, but it is not paid until the conclusion of the case.

> *Typically a contingency fee will amount to one-third of the final settlement, but it is not paid until the conclusion of the case.*

C. Won't My Insurance Company Handle the Case?

If you sustain an injury as a result of someone else's negligence (such as drunk or inattentive driving, speeding, falling on stairs, etc.), any insurance company will try to keep its cost to a minimum. You will likely be asked to sign a release form and give a statement as soon as possible. You may also be offered a settlement proposal from the at-fault party's insurer soon after the event. Although it might be tempting to sign papers or give statements as requested, here are some important points to keep in mind:

1. It is not uncommon for the full effects of traumatic injury to take days, weeks, months, or longer to show up after the initial trauma.

2. Once you have signed the insurance company's release, the matter is final. If medical or financial problems develop later, you will have no recourse to reopen your claim. All expenses related to the accident will be yours to bear alone.

3. Until your doctor believes your recovery is complete and prepares a final report stating that you have returned to pre-injury condition or that your injuries are permanent, you cannot be certain of what kinds of trauma-related medical expenses you may incur in the future.

4. If the injury was caused by another person's negligence, you are entitled to compensation for your pain and suffering, medical care, wage loss, and other financial losses. It is unlikely that the insurance company will voluntarily offer this information to you or provide reasonable compensation for your losses.

D. How Long Will it Take to Settle?

It is best not to rush settlement of your traumatic injury case. The final release that you sign when you receive your settlement check is exactly that--final! For this reason, your attorney should advise you not to settle until your doctors say your recovery is complete or the full effects of your injury are known. Negotiations with the insurance company will begin shortly after your attorney is advised by your doctors that you have either returned to pre-injury condition or that you have reached maximum medical improvement and no additional treatment will improve your condition.

> *Your attorney should advise you not to settle until your doctors say your recovery is complete or the full effects of your injury are known.*

If the Statute of Limitations dates (see pages 110–113) come up before you conclude your treatment, the attorney you hired will file a lawsuit to preserve your claim should the insurance company refuse to settle. Typical court calendars will put a date for trial one to two years from the time a lawsuit is filed.

E. What Will the Attorney Do for Me or My Family?

1. **The initial confidential consultation**. During this meeting, the attorney will obtain information from you about the cause of the trauma and your injuries. He or she will advise you of your legal rights and answer your questions. The attorney will discuss whether or not you need to hire an attorney. You should feel free to ask whatever questions you or your family think appropriate during this consultation and take notes. Ideally, bring a friend or a family member to the meeting with you. They can take notes so you are free to listen and participate fully in the meeting.

2. **Obtain legal and medical information.** If you decide to hire an attorney, he/she will gather the police report, interview the police officer(s), talk to witnesses, obtain insurance information, obtain medical records, conduct research, and perform a host of other activities. He/she will be in touch with eye witnesses, co-workers, health care providers, investigators, and experts. The attorney can concentrate on these aspects of preparing your case while you concentrate on your rehabilitation and recovery.

3. **Coordinate insurance benefits.** An attorney will collect information from the individual or family members about any insurance in effect at the time of the injury. This might include all automobile insurance, health or medical insurance, homeowner's coverage, private disability policies, work-related disability policies, and/or umbrella insurance policies.

4. **Make recommendations.** The attorney should make appropriate recommendations about actions that need to be taken to protect your interests. For example, all liability issues must be understood, and critical facts and evidence preserved. It may be necessary to interview witnesses or hire an accident reconstructionist or private investigator early on to accomplish this. Recommendations may also be made regarding who to hire as expert witnesses, and when, in preparation of the case. All this would be done by your attorney.

5. **Case evaluation and settlement negotiations.** After all important information is obtained and your health care providers have determined that you have reached pre-injury condition or you are at maximum medical improvement, a settlement letter, known as a "demand letter," is written and sent to the responsible insurance company. The demand letter includes the facts of the trauma, your traumatic injury, and how your condition has impacted your life. It also requests a monetary amount to settle your case. The attorney then negotiates with the insurance company about the amount of money you should receive to close the claim. Many claims may settle at this stage in the process. If, however, the insurance company refuses to admit responsi-

bility or compensate you fairly, a lawsuit might then be filed. This should be done only with your consent.

6. **Starting a lawsuit.** In Washington state, traumatic injury claims fall within the rules governing personal injury laws. One rule requires that if a personal injury case is not settled within three years from the date of negligence, then a lawsuit must be filed in the trial court in order to preserve your rights under the Statute of Limitations laws. See pages 110–113 for a more comprehensive discussion on the Statute of Limitations laws. A lawsuit begins when an attorney prepares legal documents, called a Summons and Complaint, files it with the trial court, and then has the papers "served" (hand delivered) to the at-fault party.

7. **Discovery, disclosure of evidence, and trial.** "Discovery" is a set of legal procedures designed to allow each party to uncover, or discover, the other party's evidence, claims, and defenses. Should the case still not settle and trial becomes necessary, your attorney will provide professional guidance and assistance every step of the way.

F. What Should I Expect When Hiring an Attorney?

At a minimum, you should expect the attorney to have experience and specialization in personal injury claims, with specific experience in the area of traumatic injury that you have experienced. Your relationship with the attorney should be comfortable for you. You should feel that your questions are answered completely.

Attorneys tend to specialize in specific areas of practice. While some may handle medical malpractice, others may specialize in auto collisions, brain trauma, roadway hazards and design, construction site defects, Workman's Compensation, etc.

Once you have decided to hire an attorney, you will sign a contract setting out the terms of legal representation. You should read this contract and ask about any provisions you do not fully understand. Signing the contract initiates legal representation, and the attorney is then empowered to begin work on your behalf.

G. A Couple of Don'ts

1. For your traumatic injury case do not hire the attorney that previously handled a family or friend's divorce case or your real estate transaction. You do not want to hire an attorney that handles cases in several areas of law – you need legal counsel that practices exclusively in personal injury law, with specific expertise in traumatic injury cases. You need and deserve a focused specialist, not a generalist.

2. Do not contact the first attorney whose advertisement you have seen on television. Although this attorney may handle hundreds of personal injury cases, such as slip and falls or whiplash claims, you have no way of knowing about his or her experience in handling traumatic injury cases. Any attorney can advertise on television. Please read pages 124–126 on lawyer advertising.

H. Attorney Interview Questions

Many lawyers do not have sufficient education, knowledge, or experience to be able to analyze, understand, prepare, and present a claim for compensation on behalf of a traumatically injured person. Just as a person with a traumatic injury needs specialized health care and treatment, they also need specialized legal representation.

Ask questions of any attorney you are considering as legal counsel to determine his/her level of experience in handling traumatic injury cases.

Here are a handful of questions to review with the attorney you are thinking about hiring to represent you.

1. How long have you been practicing law?

2. How many similar cases have you been involved with over the past three years?

3. What percentage of your law practice is devoted to similar cases and injuries?

4. What were the outcomes of your last five cases involving injuries similar to mine?

5. How do you keep up with the latest developments in traumatic injury research?

6. How many seminars or conferences have you attended over the past three years involving presentations on injuries similar to mine?

7. How many articles have you written over the past three years involving any aspect of traumatic injury?

You do not want to hire an attorney that handles cases in several areas of law.

You need and deserve a focused specialist, not a generalist.

Do not contact the first attorney whose advertisement you have seen on television.

Any attorney can advertise on television.

8. Would you and the law firm be willing to spend in advance as much as $50,000 to $100,000 or more in the investigation, preparation, and presentation of my case, if necessary?

9. What experts do you anticipate hiring to assist in the analysis and presentation of my case? (Have the attorney name any experts in the fields of neuropsychology, neurology, radiology, forensic psychiatry, chiropractic, rehabilitation, accident reconstruction, counseling, economics, cognitive therapy).

10. How accessible will you be to me if I have questions?

11. What is the hardest part about my case?

12. How will you keep me informed about my case?

13. Have you ever been disciplined by your state bar association?

14. What is your Martindale-Hubbell rating? (See page 123 for more information on this attorney-peer review rating system)

15. Which text books and/or publications do you regularly refer to when discussing traumatic injury cases?

I. Things to Consider During or After Interviewing the Attorney

1. Make sure you, the injured person, are comfortable talking with and confiding in this attorney.

2. Is the attorney fully and directly answering your questions and concerns?

3. How thoroughly has the attorney reviewed the facts of your case and injuries before giving you specific advice?

4. The level of service you have experienced through the initial process of contacting and meeting the attorney should provide some indication of the level of service you can expect throughout the case. Does it leave you with a confident feeling that you and your case will be well taken care of?

5. What do former clients of this attorney and law firm have to say? Online sites such as www.avvo.com provide additional information for you about this.

J. The Wrong Attorney

What can you do once you realize that the attorney you hired displays either inexperience, disinterest, or incompetence in handling your traumatic injury claim? You can either try to work things out with him or her, or you can change attorneys. The contingency fee agreement that you signed, which is standard in personal injury cases, does not bind the client to the attorney forever. Attorneys can be substituted at any point in the process. Many clients refrain from switching attorneys out of misplaced fear that their legal fees would increase by hiring a new attorney. The contingency fee for the attorney is generally not increased, but allocated between the first and second attorney, usually by agreement on a pro-rata basis of the amount of work done. If the former and current attorneys cannot work it out, then a court can be asked to determine the reasonable division of the contingency fee at the conclusion of the case.

Generally, you should not be asked to pay for the first attorney's time directly out of your pocket if you choose to switch. The most important thing is to make sure the attorney representing you is the one you want and trust.

K. "AV" Rating for Attorneys: What Does it Mean to You?

When an attorney notes that he or she has the "highest rating" or is "AV" rated, they are referring to the Martindale-Hubbell directory of attorneys. Martindale-Hubbell is a comprehensive guide to attorneys that independently rates their performance and no one can pay for a high rating. You can think of them as *Consumer Reports* for attorneys.

According to Martindale-Hubbell policy, its "AV" Rating is typically initiated in five-year intervals after an attorney's admission to the Bar. They request confidential opinions from other attorneys in the same geographic area. Typically, Martindale-Hubbell contacts more than 400,000 individuals to establish or confirm ratings for over 115,000 attorneys each year.

The rating process is intended as a strong indicator of an attorney's ethical standards and professional ability and is used by other attorneys when seeking a co-counsel in different jurisdictions. This rating can also be used by smart consumers in their hiring decisions.

The legal ability rating takes into consideration the standard of ability for the area in which the lawyer practices. The legal ability ratings are C'good to high; B'high to very high; and A'very high to preeminent.

The general ethical standards rating covers standards of conduct, ethics, reliability, diligence, and other criteria relevant to the discharge of professional responsibilities. The general ethical standards rating is V'very high.

An attorney who advertises that he or she is AV Rated, has been judged by his or her attorney peers to have "very high to preeminent legal ability" (A) and very high ethical standards (V). The percentage of attorneys with an AV rating practicing personal injury law is approximately 1 percent.

It is important to note that Martindale-Hubbell says that the absence of a rating should not be interpreted disfavorably toward an attorney as there can be a valid reason why an attorney may not have a rating.

L. When Do You Not Need an Attorney?

1. No personal injuries. For most situations involving only auto property damage claims, you can generally achieve an acceptable resolution on your own.

2. Mild or short duration injuries. When medical expenses are low and you have recovered quickly to pre-injury condition, then you may be able to resolve your case on your own.

M. Lawyer Advertising and What You Need to Know

Lawyer advertising for personal injury and traumatic injury cases is widespread in the Yellow Pages, TV, and in paid internet ads. It wasn't always like this. In fact, it wasn't until 1977 that a precedent-setting case from the United State Supreme Court permitted lawyer advertising. It started when a couple of attorneys in the state of Arizona advertised "low prices." Advertising had not been done previously as it was deemed unprofessional by all Bar associations. As a result of the low prices ad by these two attorneys, the bar association for the State of Arizona tried to ban their ads and other Arizona attorneys then joined the Bar's efforts to end the advertising. Litigation went all the way to the United States Supreme Court, pitting an attorney's First Amendment rights of free speech against the Arizona Bar Association's right to regulate the conduct of attorneys. The Supreme Court in *Bates v. State of Arizona*[1] ruled in 1977 that lawyer advertising is permitted in routine legal matters. This was later expanded to include personal injury cases. But, as with any type of advertising, how do you sift through all the spin and all the claims made in the advertisement? Here are some considerations when evaluating lawyer advertising.

> *The Washington State Bar Association prohibits an attorney from calling themselves a specialist and does not recognize self-proclaimed titles as such personal injury specialist.*

1. Personal Injury Specialist: The Washington State Bar Association *prohibits* an attorney from calling themselves a specialist and does not recognize self-proclaimed titles as such personal injury specialist. The only types of attorney

---

1   433 U.S. 350 (1977)

specialists recognized by the Bar Association are in the areas of taxation and patents.

2. The ability to advertise in the subject area does not mean that the attorney has the experience and training for your case.

Any attorney can advertise on any subject area. Simply stated, not all lawyers who advertise in the Yellow Pages, on television, or on the internet have real-world experience in handling the kinds of cases that they claim to handle. Personal injury attorneys do not all have the same training or experience.

There is a tremendous amount of difference from one attorney to the next. For example, did you know there are many attorneys that advertise in the area of personal injury but have never gone to a single trial? But, as a consumer, you may not know that by looking at the ads. It's a good idea to look behind the curtain to learn more about the attorney's experience and training.

3. The bigger the Yellow Page ad does *not* mean the better the attorney. Many of the personal injury attorneys that buy Yellow Pages ads, advertise on buses, or run endless TV advertisements also have a volume practice. Insurance adjusters refer to these firms as mills. The claims adjusters know that they can settle a pending case for pennies on the dollar, because that kind of law firm is designed to settle just about every case as quickly as possible. This is a shameful business practice, but their advertising strategies appear to work, since they continue to advertise and spend a lot of money doing so.

4. Internet Searches: The first, second or third hit in an internet search are generally a result of paid placements or advertising, and have nothing to do with the attorney's training or experience. These are also known as sponsored links, which can be located at the top of the search results or on the right hand side of the screen. These sites do not screen for the attorney's qualifications. Attorneys pay a fee or per click rate to position their listing in the first, second, or third tier of a search.

5. Some ads tout that the "combined experience" of the law firm is thirty years. But what if the five attorneys working together each has only six years. Is that sufficient experience to handle your case? Steer clear of ads that talk about combined experience.

6. If the ad sounds too slick, it is.

When searching for the right attorney on your case ask around and get referrals. Word-of-mouth recommendations from people that you know and trust are the best way to start. Then contact the attorney and have an initial consultation before deciding whether to hire the attorney. Review the Interview Questions that I have provided on pages 120–122. And don't be shy about asking the questions before selecting your attorney. If the attorney does not answer your questions, hedges his or her answers clearly, or is unwilling to do so, then chances are they're not the right attorney for you. Make sure you get a good feeling from him or her and are comfortable with the attorney you choose. After all, you will be working together for months to come on issues that are important to you and your loved ones.

PART THREE

YOUR ROAD
TO PHYSICAL RECOVERY

Introduction to Traumatic Injuries —
Not All Injuries Heal 100%

CHAPTER 31

The good news: Traumatic injuries can heal without any residual problems. The bad news: a significant percentage of those who suffer a traumatic injury will continue to experience residual symptoms even after being released from active treatment.

The greater the impact that this permanent condition has on your loss of work, home life, and recreational activities, then the higher the value of your claim.

Many insurers will try to deny or downplay the significance or reality of continuing symptoms, particularly when the continued pain relates to the neck or back regions of the body. For example, the insurer responsible to pay compensation to the injured party for a permanent and ongoing condition will argue that only limited short-term care is required unless there was evidence of a joint injury, surgery, or disc herniation.

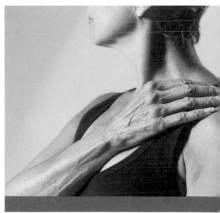

©Fancy Photography/Veer

They will argue that the injury is merely soft tissue and that all soft tissue issues resolve fully without any permanent condition, heal spontaneously, and do not require treatment. However, there are many studies showing that soft tissue injuries can cause long-term neck or back problems. Additionally, the injuries may not be soft tissue in nature, but rather to the disc or facet joints of the spine. See page 142 for a discussion of facet joints injuries and how this can lead to ongoing pain issues.

In one study published in the *Journal of Bone and Joint Surgery,* the authors followed up on patients involved in motor vehicle collisions approximately fifteen years earlier.[1] The authors wanted to know whether patients, fifteen years after cervical injury, had improved or worsened symptoms, and whether psychological variables played a role in the patient's condition. A group of sixty-one patients was studied. All had presented to the same emergency department in England after car collision-related soft tissue injury to the neck. Forty were available for the follow-up. Ninety percent of this group had been involved in rear-end motor vehicle collisions.

The patients were questioned about symptoms and underwent physical examinations. Psychological assessments were also performed. The authors came to many noteworthy conclusions, including:

* Seventy percent of the patients still had symptoms fifteen years after a whiplash injury. Of the 70 percent, 42 percent (more than one-half) had moderate to severe symptoms impacting their daily activities while 28 percent had mild symptoms not considered intrusive into one's ability to function.

* Although 18 percent had improved over the past five years, a greater number of 28 percent had worsened.

* Older patients were more likely to continue to experience symptoms, and only 5 percent of those who were over age 40 at the time of the collision were free from symptoms in follow up.

* Symptoms did *not* improve after conclusion of their claims.

* The pain maps explained previously published views that radiating pain is associated with more severe impairment and disability.

* The distribution of pain conformed more closely to radiation from the facet joints rather than from nerve pathways.

---

1   Squires, B.; Gargan M.F.; Bannister, G.C., ASoft Tissues Injuries of the Cervical Spine: A 15 year Follow-up,@ *Journal of Bone and Joint Surgery,* Vol. 78-B, No. 6, November 1996, pp. 955.57.

＊ An abnormal psychological profile in patients with symptoms after fifteen years suggested a correlation between chronic pain and depressive symptoms.

It is important to note that this study was unable to determine whether depressive symptoms were the result or cause of chronic pain, although subsequent published medical literature has more often found depression and anxiety about traumatic injury to be *caused* by living with chronic pain, consistent with most patients' subjective experiences.

Though studies are useful to provide a basis for establishing that musculoskeletal injuries result in chronic problems, explaining why it occurs is of critical importance in a traumatic injury case. Your traumatic injury can potentially result in long-term pain and needs to be fully evaluated by the best health care providers, often from different areas of specialization. For example, your primary care physician's assessment, diagnosis, and explanation of the ongoing cause of pain may be different from other providers such as a chiropractors, spine specialists, neurologists, or surgeons. Having multiple health care providers weigh-in with their opinions, may provide the type of evidence to establish the validity of your ongoing symptoms. Afterall, the insurance company on the opposite side of your claim will have access to hired gun doctors from different specialities trying to discredit you, your treatment expenses, and your doctors' opinions.

Necks and Car Crashes: A Bad Combination

CHAPTER 32

The neck is a very complex structure.

Many medical researchers and health care providers have noted that the neck's structure is more vulnerable and subject to injury than any other portion of the spine. The neck is placed between the thoracic (mid-back) spine, which is relatively immobile, and the skull, a weight that must be balanced on the cervical spine and held in place by the supporting capsular, ligamentous, cartilaginous, and muscular structures.

Physical laws dictate that rear-end auto collisions produce a sudden acceleration which is transmitted through the car seat to the occupant's body.

The combination of an eight to twelve pound head (think bowling ball) on top of a highly flexible neck results in the potential injury of the neck, as the body is suddenly accelerated forward.

This abnormal movement of the neck has been most carefully studied with simulated rear impact collisions, as well as in biomechanics laboratories with live human subjects. Since the mid-1990s, previous conventional wisdom about this movement involving a simple hyperextension (i.e., bending back) of the neck has been challenged. More contemporary research suggests that the head actually tilts downward, not upward, although the lower part of the neck is in hyperextension, causing a sort of S-shaped curve to the neck when viewed from the

RICHARD H. ADLER
Attorney at Law, Adler Giersch PS

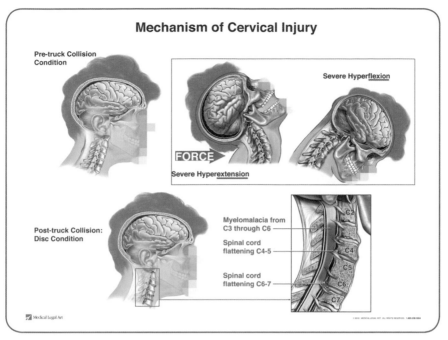

Mechanism of Cervical Injury

Pre-truck Collision Condition

Severe Hyperflexion

FORCE

Severe Hyperextension

Post-truck Collision: Disc Condition

Myelomalacia from C3 through C6

Spinal cord flattening C4-5

Spinal cord flattening C6-7

C2
C4
C5
C6
C7

Medical Legal Art

©1997-2010 Medical Legal Art. www.doereport.com

side. In addition, the head, when subjected to rear-end impact tends to retract backwards until it contacts the head rest of the car seat. A greater distance of retracting backwards correlates to an increased probability of neck injury. There is a second phase where the head and neck together are jerked forward (think of touching your chin to your chest) as a mechanical backlash to the initial event, possibly aided by bouncing of the head against the head restraint and reflex contraction of the neck muscles. This type of injury tends to stretch and tear the soft tissues that limit extension (going backward) and flexion (going forward) of the neck.

Insurance adjusters are trained to argue that the nature and extent of traumatic injuries rests solely on the extent of damage to the vehicle. This practice is misleading and inaccurate; it fails to take into account significant variables such as road surface conditions, speed, acceleration of the vehicles, size and weight of the vehicles, position of head restraints, mechanical stiffness of the vehicle and the occupant's seat, age, gender of the occu-

> *Insurance adjusters are trained to argue that the nature and extent of traumatic injuries rests solely on the extent of damage to the vehicle.*

pants, element of surprise, and position of the body and head at the time of impact. Each of these factors affects the degree of severity of an injury. Let's examine a few variables.

Road Surface Conditions

The acceleration of a car struck from behind can be closely *estimated*, but not exactly measured by a mathematical formula to determine the amount of force produced during a collision. These forces by themselves do not measure the true acceleration. A number of other variables may be involved in any particular collision, affecting the degree of force exerted on the occupant's body, including whether the road surface is wet or dry.

Velocity

When a vehicle is rear-ended it is accelerated forward. It is a well-established principle that sudden acceleration caused by a rear-end impact exerts even greater G-forces on the head and the cervical spine than on the struck vehicle.

To get a better idea of how much force and acceleration were generated in a rear-end collision, an engineer or accident reconstructionist would ask:

* What distance did the struck vehicle move after impact?

* Were road conditions wet, dry, or icy?

* Was the driver braking at the time of impact?

* Were items inside the vehicle thrown about?

* Did the impact knock off the occupant's glasses or hat?

Size and Weight of Vehicle

The relative size of colliding vehicles is also an important variable in determining the extent of injury. For example, a streetcar traveling at a speed of 3 mph will produce the same amount of damage and acceleration force as a compact car traveling at 40 mph[1] simply because it weighs so much more.

---

1   Rothman & Simone, The Spine, "Acceleration Extension Injuries of the Cervical Spine" by Ian McNabb, Vol. II, 2nd ed., 1982, p.654

Head Restraints

Head restraints are designed to limit the backward displacement of the head during the acceleration phase of whiplash. Head restraints should be adjusted so that the center is level with the ears. This is about the center point of gravity for the head. During the acceleration phase of the whiplash, the torso is forced backward against the seat back and at the same time may shift upward. This may allow the head to slide up and above the head restraint especially if it is positioned too low. This phenomenon is known as "ramping" and it will increase neck injuries.

Another important variable to consider is the distance between the occupant's head and the restraint at the time of impact. This distance can be affected by the posture of the occupant and by the degree of seat back inclination (how upright or reclined your seat is). The bigger this distance, the less effective the head restraint.

Verity Jane Smith/Brand X Pictures/Getty Images

Age

Range of motion in the cervical spine decreases with age, just as the supporting soft tissue become less elastic. Strength of the neck musculature also diminishes with age. Over the adult life span, cervical range of motion is reduced, cervical muscle reflexes slow, and voluntary strength capability diminishes by 25 percent. This loss of flexibility and strength significantly increases the potential for serious injury.

Rotated Head

The likelihood of a severe injury is greater when uneven loads are applied to the spine. This can occur when a vehicle is struck in the left-rear corner, as it is turning, or when the occupant's head is turned to the side while gazing out a window or talking to another occupant. When the head is rotated 45 degrees, the neck's ability to extend backwards is decreased by 50 percent. This results in increased forces on the joints on one side and different forces on the other. The spaces in the spine through which the nerves pass are smaller when the head is turned, making the nerves more vulnerable to injury.

INJURIES:
HARD V. SOFT TISSUE
CHAPTER 33

There are as many types of injuries as there are ways to be injured. Two patients with identical diagnoses may have widely different symptoms and pain experiences. This is because there are many different types of structures in and around each joint of the body.

Before examining each type of structure, we can simply start by dividing the body into hard and soft tissue. The body is made up of hard tissue (bone, teeth) and soft tissues (muscle, tendon, ligament, facet joint cartilage, disc, etc.).

Hard tissue injuries are much easier to see than soft tissue. On imaging tests, for example, a bone fracture can easily be seen on X-ray as hard tissue breaks, but soft tissue stretches and tears are more difficult to visualize, and as a result, can be more difficult to properly locate and treat.

The most common diagnostic imaging test used immediately after trauma is the X-ray, since the initial concern is whether any bones are fractured, which can lead to serious medical consequences. Soft tissues, however, do not appear well on X-rays and, as a result, do not provide an accurate picture or diagnosis of which structures may be damaged.

A common and much misunderstood injury is "whiplash." While this is slang to describe the type of soft-tissue injury frequently suffered in rear-end car accidents, the term is imprecise, and is neither a medical term nor a proper medical diagnosis. Whiplash is a term often used by insurers to distort a real injury so that the average layperson will believe that a physician has overtreated or that an injured party is exaggerating. A more accurate description of the type of injury referred to as whiplash is an "acceleration-deceleration," "hyperextension/hyperflexion," or "an S-shaped compression curve" injury to the cervical spine (see pages 132–135 for more discussion on this).

A proper understanding of the mechanisms of the hyperextension/hyperflexion injury helps explain how and why specific structures in the neck or back (muscles, ligaments, nerves, discs, facets) are traumatically injured. Serious consequences can develop from soft tissue injuries: cerebral concussion, damage to the cartilage in the cervical area, protrusions or herniation of discs, or aggravation of a pre-existing condition are common examples. Medical literature now recognizes that soft tissue injuries can be disabling and result in permanent problems. In one study, 62 percent of the patients who had traditional medical care, including referral to a specialist, continued to have symptoms twelve years after their personal injury case was resolved.[1] In another study, 12 percent of patients who had suffered hyperextension/hyperflexion injury were still significantly disabled several years after injury. There is radiographic (x-ray) evidence that a whiplash victim is about 6.5 times more likely than the general population to develop degenerative disc disease in the seven-year period following injury.[2] These are important factors for an attorney to understand and bring to light during the case in order to negotiate a better resolution.

Soft tissue injuries heal in three phases. The initial phase is inflammation: pain, swelling, redness, and warmth.

The next phase is known as the repair phase and can last for several weeks.

The last phase is known as the remodeling phase.

In general, soft tissue injuries heal in three phases. The initial phase is inflammation: pain, swelling, redness, and warmth. This can last for several days or longer. During this period of time the body creates collagen and begins to lay it down across and around the injured area. This collagen creates scar tissue as a way to tie together the weakened areas. Without proper manual mobili-

---

1   S.P. Hudgson and M. Gundy, "Whiplash Injuries: Their Long Term Prognosis and its Relationship to Compensation," Neuro-Orthopedics, Vol. 7, 1989, pp. 88-91

2   M.F. Gargan and G.C. Bannister, "Prognostic Factors in Soft Tissue Injuries of the Cervical Spine," J. Bone Joint Surgery (br.), Vol. 72B, 1990, pp. 901-903

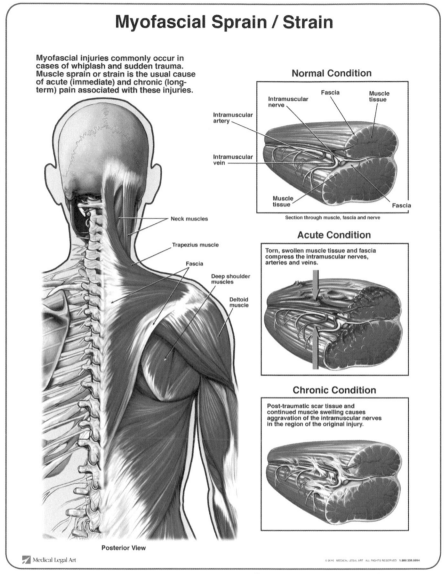

Myofascial Sprain / Strain

Myofascial injuries commonly occur in cases of whiplash and sudden trauma. Muscle sprain or strain is the usual cause of acute (immediate) and chronic (long-term) pain associated with these injuries.

Normal Condition

Intramuscular nerve
Fascia
Muscle tissue
Intramuscular artery
Intramuscular vein
Muscle tissue
Fascia

Section through muscle, fascia and nerve

Neck muscles
Trapezius muscle
Fascia
Deep shoulder muscles
Deltoid muscle

Acute Condition

Torn, swollen muscle tissue and fascia compress the intramuscular nerves, arteries and veins.

Chronic Condition

Post-traumatic scar tissue and continued muscle swelling causes aggravation of the intramuscular nerves in the region of the original injury.

Posterior View

Medical Legal Art

© 2010 MEDICAL LEGAL ART. ALL RIGHTS RESERVED. 1.800.338.5954

zation from a chiropractor, physical therapist, and/or massage therapist during this critical period, scar tissue will likely form in a way that causes permanent restrictions on joint motion and sensitivity. The last phase is known as the remodeling phase. This is also a critical period as the collagen produced by the body will be used to replicate the damaged tissue. Again, proper rehabilitation from a chiropractor, physical therapist, and/or massage therapist during this period is essential for proper healing. This phase may take several weeks to more than a year or longer depending on the nature of the injury; likewise, your treatments may last several weeks to a year.

What is initially diagnosed as a hyperextension/hyperflexion injury may ultimately result in a much more focused diagnosis. Hyperextension/hyperflexion injury includes any soft-tissue injury that results from a specific type of traumatic force – a rear-end collision. However, the specific structures of the spine that were injured vary from person to person; therefore, not all injuries with this diagnosis can be treated identically.

THE SPINE

Musculoskeletal injuries include any injury to the different structures that make up the spine; these include vertebrae, facets, discs, ligaments, tendons, muscles, and tissue.

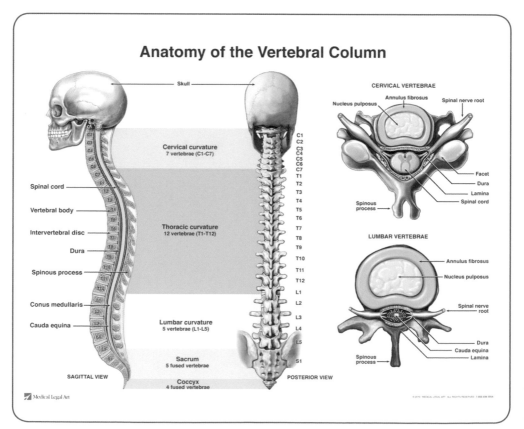

Anatomy of the Vertebral Column

Skull

Cervical curvature
7 vertebrae (C1-C7)

Spinal cord

Vertebral body

Intervertebral disc

Dura

Spinous process

Conus medullaris

Cauda equina

Thoracic curvature
12 vertebrae (T1-T12)

Lumbar curvature
5 vertebrae (L1-L5)

Sacrum
5 fused vertebrae

Coccyx
4 fused vertebrae

SAGITTAL VIEW

C1
C2
C3
C4
C5
C6
C7
T1
T2
T3
T4
T5
T6
T7
T8
T9
T10
T11
T12
L1
L2
L3
L4
L5
S1

POSTERIOR VIEW

CERVICAL VERTEBRAE

Annulus fibrosus

Nucleus pulposus

Spinal nerve root

Spinous process

Facet

Dura

Lamina

Spinal cord

LUMBAR VERTEBRAE

Annulus fibrosus

Nucleus pulposus

Spinal nerve root

Spinous process

Dura

Cauda equina

Lamina

Medical Legal Art

The most frequent musculoskeletal injuries involve areas in the neck and low back. The number of parts and the complexity of the spinal column often make the initial determination of the exact injury difficult to pinpoint, as injury to different structures can have similar symptoms at onset. Let's take a closer look at the different structures in the spine and how they relate to one another.

a. Vertebrae

The spine is made up of thirty-three bones (vertebrae) stacked upon one another. The neck is made up of the seven top vertebrae, known as the cervical spine.

The next twelve vertebrae make up the thoracic spine. The lumbar spine is comprised of five vertebrae. The sacrum is comprised of five vertebrae, and the coccyx is made up of four. The vertebrae of the sacrum and the coccyx are fused together. Each level of the spine is numbered from the top down. For example, C-7 stands for the cervical vertebrae, seventh down from the skull. L-4 means the lumbar vertebra and it is the fourth from the top of the lumbar part of the spinal column.

b. Spinal Cord

The spinal vertebrae protect the spinal cord, which runs through a hole behind each vertebrae of the spine. The spinal cord starts at the bottom of the brain in an area called the brain stem and runs all the way down to the area of the sacrum at the bottom of the spine. The spinal cord is housed in a tube containing cerebral spinal fluid (CSF). The spinal cord runs down your spine behind the discs at the back side of the vertebra. Nerves from the spinal cord exit the sides of the spinal column through holes (the foramina) between the stacked vertebra. These nerves branch out from the spinal cord throughout the body, carrying instructions from the brain that allows you to move your hands, walk, talk, breathe, etc.

> *The spinal cord runs down your spine behind the discs at the back side of the vertebra. Nerves from the spinal cord exit the sides of the spinal column through holes at each vertebra.*

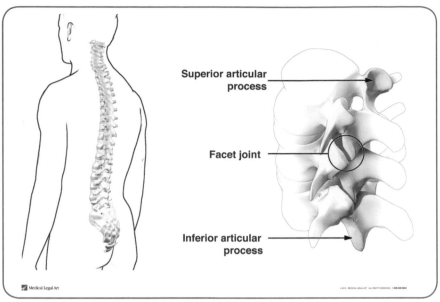

©1997-2010 Medical Legal Art. www.doereport.com

c. Facet

Joints on either side of the vertebrae, called the facet joints, connect the vertebrae to each other. The facet is on the back and to the side of the vertebra and holds it in place, but also allows for movement such as twisting and rotating.

Facet joints, like all joints in the body, have a thin cartilage lining that allow them to move easily. These joints and their cartilage can be damaged by traumatic injuries, disrupting the normal motion of the spinal joint. Trauma can lead to damage of the cartilage and/or nerve endings, resulting in inflammation of the joint, and cause decreased joint motion and increased pain.

Symptoms of pain from the facet joints can be difficult to diagnose as they often mimic the symptoms of a strain or sprain of soft tissues such as tendons or ligaments. If conservative treatment of chiropractic, physical therapy, acupuncture, and/or massage do not result in substantial resolution of the symptoms, your healthcare provider may recommend a facet injection.

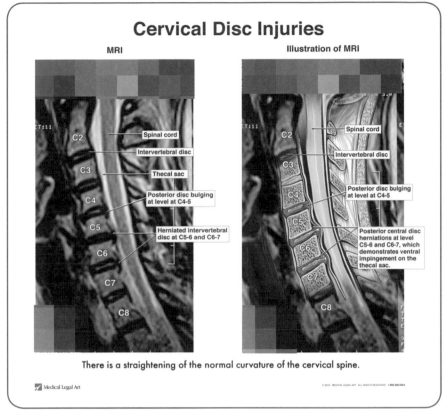

Cervical Disc Injuries

MRI

Illustration of MRI

Spinal cord

C2

Intervertebral disc

C3

Thecal sac

Posterior disc bulging
at level at C4-5

C4

C5

Herniated intervertebral
disc at C5-6 and C6-7

C6

C7

C8

Spinal cord

C2

Intervertebral disc

C3

Posterior disc bulging
at level at C4-5

C4

C5

Posterior central disc
herniations at level
C5-6 and C6-7, which
demonstrates ventral
impingement on the
thecal sac.

C6

C7

C8

There is a straightening of the normal curvature of the cervical spine.

Medical Legal Art

d. Disc: Herniations and Protrusions

Between each vertebrae is a gel-filled, fibrous ring called a disc. The disc is shaped like a kidney bean and is in front of the spinal cord. The outside, fibrous portion of the disc is called the *annulus fibrosis*. The gel-like substance within the disc is the *nucleus pulposus*. The disc acts as a shock absorber between the vertebrae. An injury to the disc can cause disruption of the joint and interference with spinal nerves or normal joint function and wear.

A disc can be injured in several different ways. For example, the outer ring of the disc (*annulus fibrosis*), can become torn, allowing the inner gel-like substance (*nucleus pulposus*) to leak out. This is known as a *herniated disc* and it can press upon the spinal canal or on the nerves exiting through the openings in the vertebrae. The pressure on the nerves causes pain at the level of the herniation, but also commonly radiates out from the area. This radiating pain can be accompanied

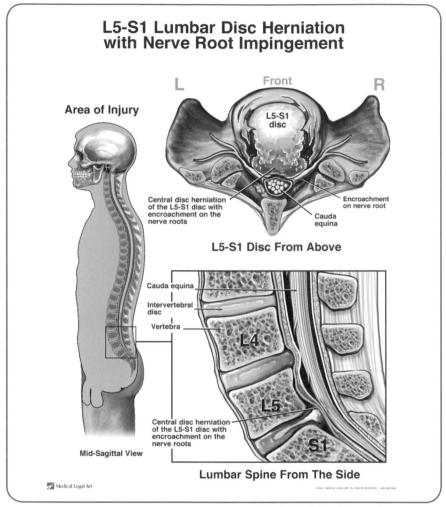

L5-S1 Lumbar Disc Herniation with Nerve Root Impingement

L   Front   **R**

Area of Injury

L5-S1 disc

Central disc herniation of the L5-S1 disc with encroachment on the nerve roots

Encroachment on nerve root

Cauda equina

L5-S1 Disc From Above

Cauda equina

Intervertebral disc

Vertebra

L4

Central disc herniation of the L5-S1 disc with encroachment on the nerve roots

L5

S1

Mid-Sagittal View

Medical Legal Art

Lumbar Spine From The Side

by numbness, tingling, and weakness and can extend as far as the affected nerve travels along the pathway down the arms or legs.

A disc herniation in the low back can cause pain extending down the leg and into the foot. A disc herniation in the neck can cause symptoms extending into the arms and hands.

In the past, it was believed that a disc herniation itself could not cause pain without interference with a nearby nerve. However, recent medical studies have proven that the disc itself contains nerve fibers or nerve endings that connect to the underside of the vertebrae. A tear in these fibers, known as the *hyperintensity zone* (HIZ), will cause pain, even when the discs do not appear to interfere with a nerve.

A disc injury can also cause pain when the disc is not herniated or ruptured. In this situation, the disc is not torn, but extends outward, beyond its normal area. This is known as a *disc bulge*.

A disc protrusion or bulge is very different than a disc herniation. A protruding or bulging disc occurs when the inner gel-like center (*nucleus pulposes*) is squeezed in a way that stretches, but does not tear, the outer ring (*annulus fibrosus*) of the disc. A herniated, protruded, or bulged disc can press on nerves that travel to the legs or arms and can cause numbness, tingling, weakness, and/or pain. However, it is generally the herniated or leaking disc that is of most concern to your doctors.

e. Nerve Root

Nerves from the spinal cord branch out through small holes in the vertebrae at the each level, known as the foramina. The branches

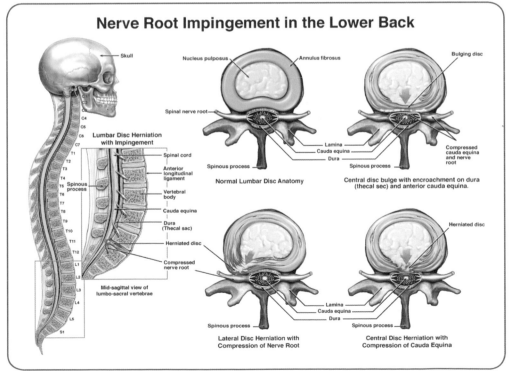

are called nerve roots and extend out to all parts of the body. This explains why a neck injury causes pain down the arm and a back injury causes pain down the leg. Also, if a disc is herniated or protruded, it can come in contact with the nerve root and put pressure on it, causing pain, numbness, and/or tingling. Some even experience a loss of strength, resulting in difficulty gripping, holding, picking up a frying pan or even a mug of coffee, foot-dragging, or weakness of quadricep muscles.

f. Ligament Injuries

A ligament is a tough, elastic band of tissue that connects bone to bone – often holding joints together. Though ligaments are somewhat elastic, they have a limit to the range they can be stretched. When a ligament is stretched beyond its normal range, it does not snap back to its normal length immediately. This can affect the proper function of the ligaments – to hold other parts in place. When this structure is not holding properly, the entire joint may experience dysfunction (imagine a sloppy, loose joint). Other structures surrounding the joint, such as muscle, may compensate for the change, resulting in muscle bracing (or spasm), attempting to tighten up the joint and hold it in place. As the ligament heals, it may be unable to return to its pre-injury length, resulting in a permanent loss of function of the ligament and, therefore, the joint. The ligament may also heal with scar tissue that can further disrupt joint function and cause continuing pain.

> *When a ligament is stretched beyond its normal range, it does not snap back to its normal length immediately. This can affect the proper function of the ligaments – to hold other parts in place.*

Normal wear-and-tear of joints is a part of aging. However, permanent stretching of a ligament following traumatic injury can result in accelerated degeneration or wear of the joint. When a joint consistently moves in an abnormal manner, the wear on the joint is increased. This wear occurs more quickly in the injured joint than in the normal healthy joint, and can lead to significant problems.

g. Tendon

A tendon is a band of strong tissue connecting muscle to bone and, if stretched or torn, can cause enormous pain and inflammation. Most tendon injuries occur near joints such as the shoulder, elbow, knee, and ankle. Direct trauma, such as a blow to the body received during a motor vehicle collision, can cause a tendon to rupture. Many doctors will describe a tendon injury as tendonitis (inflammation of a tendon), tendinosis (tiny tear in the tissue around the tendon, caused by overuse) or tendinopathy (a term covering both inflammation and tears). Symptoms of tendinopathy include pain and stiffness, particularly upon arising in the morning; loss of strength; tenderness, redness, and warmth, in the case of an inflamed tendon; and a "crunchy" sound or feeling when using the tendon. Treatment of tendinopathy usually involves icing and resting the injured area, easing back into the activity which caused it, physical therapy, chiropractic care, or massage treatment. In extreme cases, surgery may be called for, in which the tendon is sewn back together or a graft is placed on the tendon.

h. Muscle

A traumatic event can put sudden pressure on a muscle, causing it to strain. A strained muscle can result in swelling, bruising or redness, and/or pain. A strained muscle implies damage to a muscle or its attaching tendons.

Muscle damage from a sprain can take the form of a partial or full tear of the muscle fibers and the tendons attached to the muscle. Muscle tearing can also damage small blood vessels, causing local bleeding (bruising) and pain (caused by irritation of the nerve endings in the area).

Ice is favored early on after a strain or sprain to reduce inflammation. In the latter phase of healing when inflammation has subsided, heat or ice can be the favored treatment approach.

i. Tissue

The phrase soft tissue refers to muscles, tendons, and ligaments. A traumatic injury to soft tissues causes a similar result of pain, swelling, redness, and/or instability.

Though injuries to soft tissues are common with trauma, they cannot be seen with X-rays. As a result, it is more difficult to detect these injuries than a bone injury. Individuals with soft-tissue trauma may not experience symptoms immediately and in some situations it may take a few days. A person with soft tissue trauma and resulting pain will also experience inflammation or swelling in the area. This is the body's way of making you aware of an injury and the need to obtain proper treatment. If left untreated, the injury will inhibit proper healing.

STRAIN V. SPRAIN — DIFFERENCES

CHAPTER 35

After suffering a traumatic injury and subsequent neck or back pain, healthcare providers might diagnosis the injury as a "strain" or "sprain," often using them interchangeably. However, a strain and sprain are two different medical diagnoses.

A strain involves stretching a muscle's structure *slightly* beyond its usual range. Simple strains do not involve any long-term damage of the joint structure, but still may need treatment to resolve the pain and increase function. A sprain, on the other hand, is an injury that has stretched a joint's structures *well beyond* the normal range, resulting in tearing or stretching of tissue, ligament, (the tough fibrous tissue that connects bone to other bones), muscle, or damaging the facet or joint.

Strains and sprains are categorized as Grade I (mild), Grade II (moderate), or Grade III (severe). Strain symptoms can include muscle spasms, muscle weakness, swelling, cramping, pain, bruising, and decreased ability to move or use the injured joint.

A strain injury should heal within several weeks with no residual effects. But when a musculoskeletal injury fails to resolve within a period of weeks, it is likely that you had more than a strain injury. You may want your primary care physician or chiropractor to

> *A sprain, on the other hand, is an injury that has stretched a joint's structures well beyond the normal range, resulting in tearing or stretching of tissue, ligament, (the tough fibrous tissue that connects bone to other bones), muscle, or damaging the facet or joint.*

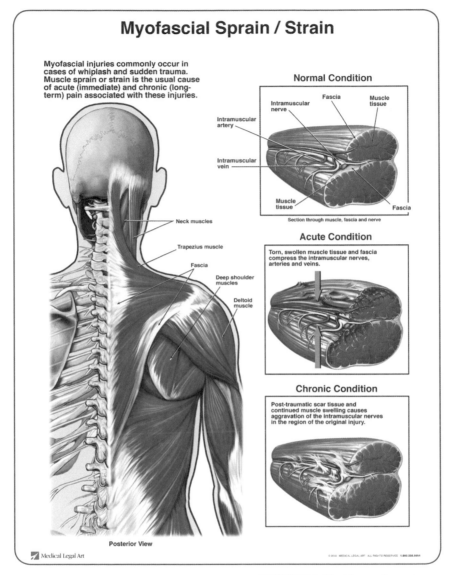

Myofascial Sprain / Strain

Myofascial injuries commonly occur in cases of whiplash and sudden trauma. Muscle sprain or strain is the usual cause of acute (immediate) and chronic (long-term) pain associated with these injuries.

Neck muscles

Trapezius muscle

Fascia

Deep shoulder muscles

Deltoid muscle

Posterior View

Normal Condition

Intramuscular nerve

Fascia

Muscle tissue

Intramuscular artery

Intramuscular vein

Muscle tissue

Fascia

Section through muscle, fascia and nerve

Acute Condition

Torn, swollen muscle tissue and fascia compress the intramuscular nerves, arteries and veins.

Chronic Condition

Post-traumatic scar tissue and continued muscle swelling causes aggravation of the intramuscular nerves in the region of the original injury.

Medical Legal Art

©1997-2010 Medical Legal Art. www.doereport.com

take a closer look to determine which structures have been injured and how these structures are most appropriately treated. Or it may be a good idea to ask your treating doctor to refer you for a second opinion. However, even a strain injury may not heal within a few weeks or even months because of scar tissue that was created and continues to cause pain and limitations. A strain can also be accompanied by other injuries to the disc or facets.

JOINT INJURIES — GENERAL

Joints are the places at which two bones come together to aid in motion. Each joint is made up of cartilage at the ends of the bone.

Joint movement ranges from none (fixed) through slight movement to highly mobile, such as the knee and elbow. Trauma can cause an injury to any joint of the body and change its natural mobility function.

Ligaments hold the joints together, while muscles attached to the joint by tendons control movement. Joint injury can involve any of the structures of the joint. When any part of the structure is injured, proper joint movement may be disrupted, either limiting the movement (hypomobile) or creating too much movement (hypermobile).

Abnormal movement of any joint on a long-term basis causes wear-and-tear on the joint. This wear can accelerate the degenerative process of the joint, leading to arthritis and greater susceptibility to future injury.

There are several types of common injuries in mobile joints. A dislocation occurs when the bone of the joint is forcibly moved out of its socket. Bones may be fractured at the ends where they form the joint. Wrenching, stretching, or tearing of the supporting structures, such as ligaments or tendons, are common. Lastly, the cartilage that lies on the bone's surface at the joint can be torn. These injuries can cause anything from minor, short-term pain to a permanent condition requiring surgery or long-term care.

Abnormal movement of any joint on a long-term basis causes wear-and-tear on the joint. This wear can accelerate the degenerative process of the joint, leading to arthritis and greater susceptibility to future injury.

KNEE JOINT INJURIES

To understand knee injuries, it is important to know how the knee works. The knee is a mobile joint between the tibia and fibula (shin bones) and the femur (thigh bone). The patella, or kneecap, sits over the front of the knee joint. Within the joint, two discs of protective cartilage, the menisci, cover the surfaces of the bones to reduce friction with movement of the shin and thigh bones.

The entire knee joint is partly encased in a fibrous capsule and lined with a synovial membrane that produces lubricating fluid, so that the knee joint can move with ease.

The shape of the knee joint provides stability, and ligaments surrounding the knee provide further support. Four ligaments on all sides of the knee limit side-to-side movement, such as the anterior cruciate ligament (ACL), the posterior cruciate ligament (PCL), the medial collateral ligament (MCL), and the lateral collateral ligament (LCL). Cruciate ligaments cross over each other between the *tibia* and *femur*. Fluid-filled sacs, called *bursa*, are present above and below the kneecap and behind the knee.

Meniscus Tear

The *meniscus*, the C-shaped disc of *cartilage* separating the *tibia* and *femur* may tear partially or fully from a traumatic injury. Symptoms of a *meniscus* tear may include a popping sound at the time of the injury,

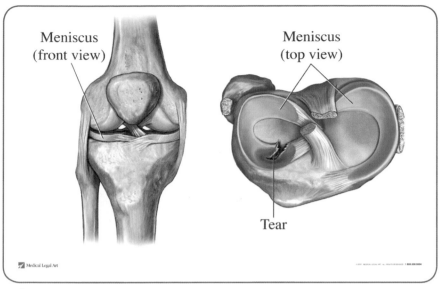

Meniscus
(front view)

Meniscus
(top view)

Tear

Medical Legal Art

©1997-2010 Medical Legal Art. www.doereport.com

pain in the knee joint (particularly in the area of the *meniscus*), joint tenderness, swelling, catching, or locking of the knee. A patient with a *meniscus* tear may find climbing up or down stairs to be painful.

Ligament Tears

Any of the ligaments surrounding the knee may be torn by trauma. There are four main ligaments that connect the tibia and femur.

Anterior Cruciate Ligament (ACL)

The ACL crosses from the front to the back of the knee; its cousin, the *posterior cruciate ligament* (PCL), crosses from the back to the front of the knee. The ACL is most commonly torn in the middle or pulled off of the femur.

There are four main ligaments that connect the tibia and femur.

A blow to the side of the knee, a sudden twisting motion of the joint, or overextending the knee are common causes of ACL injuries.

Initial symptoms of an ACL injury may include a popping

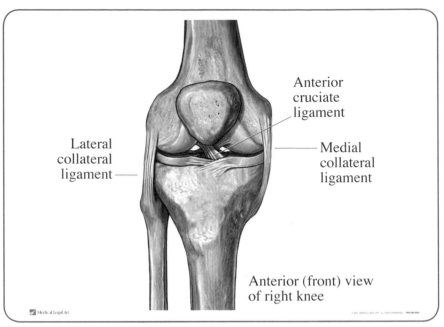

Anterior cruciate ligament

Lateral collateral ligament

Medial collateral ligament

Anterior (front) view of right knee

Medical Legal Art

©1997-2010 Medical Legal Art. www.doereport.com

sound at the time of injury, severe pain, and swelling within several hours of the injury. In the later stages of an ACL injury, the injured person may complain that the knee feels unstable or "gives out."

Posterior Cruciate Ligament (PCL)

The PCL extends from the top rear of the tibia to the bottom-front surface of the femur, providing stability to the back of the joint. Hyperextension (overextending the joint) or direct blows to the flexed knee are common causes of PCL injury. "Dashboard knee" is a common diagnosis after an automobile collision in which your knee strikes the dashboard, injuring the PCL. Symptoms of the PCL injury include joint pain, swelling, tenderness in the space behind the knee, and joint instability.

Medial Collateral Ligament (MCL)

The *medial collateral ligament* runs along the inside of the knee, from the upper-inside surface of the *tibia* (shin) to the bottom-inside surface of the *femur* (thigh). This ligament stabilizes the joint on the inside of the knee, preventing inward movement.

Injury to this ligament usually occurs as a result of external pressure on the knee joint that exerts force on the MCL. The same force can result in a traumatic injury to the ACL. Symptoms may include pain or tenderness along the inside of the kneecap, swelling and knee instability, or giving out.

Lateral Collateral Ligament (LCL)

The LCL is the counterpart of the *medial collateral ligament*. It extends from the top outside surface of the *fibia* (the bone on the outside of the lower leg) to the bottom-outside surface of the *femur* (thigh). The ligament stabilizes the knee joint.

Injury to the LCL usually occurs as a result of force exerted on the inside of the knee, placing pressure on the LCL. Symptoms may include pain or tenderness along the outside of the kneecap, swelling, and knee instability or giving out.

Assessment and Diagnosis

When you go to your doctor with a knee injury, your doctor will consider the history of injury, the symptoms, and will conduct a physical examination to come to a diagnosis. The history will include a description of how the injury occurred, the progression of the symptoms, and any symptoms or conditions of the knee prior to the injury. During a physical examination, the doctor will perform specific tests that will help establish which structures of the knee are injured.

The doctor may then order a knee joint X-ray and/or an *MRI (Magnetic Resonance Imaging)*.

X-rays will reveal any changes to the bone, alignment of the joint, or the presence of abnormal fluid in the joint. An MRI can reveal tears to the cartilage, meniscus, or ligaments of the knee joint.

Treatment

If the MRI is positive for a stretch or tear to the *ligament* or *cartilage*, then you might be referred to an orthopedic surgeon for further evaluation. Other treatment options will depend on several factors, including the severity of the tear, your age, the general condition of the remainder of the joint, and your response to treatment. Treatment may include the use of ice and nonsteroidal anti-inflammatory (NSAID) medication to reduce swelling and pain, use of a brace, and mobilization therapies from a chiropractor, physical therapist, or massage therapist.

If your knee injury does not improve following these treatments, then *arthroscopic surgery* may be necessary. This involves insertion of a small camera (less than 1/4 inch in diameter) into the knee joint to view the internal condition of the knee. When a tear or other injury is found, the surgeon may make additional small incisions to access the injured area and repair the affected structure. Follow-up may include medication to control inflammation, physical therapy, chiropractic, bracing, health care monitoring, or other instructions.

SHOULDER JOINT INJURIES

CHAPTER 38

Another joint of the body that is often associated with traumatic injuries from an automobile collision is the shoulder. It is made up of a ball (the head of the *humerus* or upper arm bone) and a socket into which the *humerus* fits.

The shoulder is made up of three main bones: the arm bone (humerus), the collarbone (clavicle), and the shoulder blade (scapula). The scapula and the clavicle come together to form the socket into which the ball of the humerus fits.

Muscles, tendons, and ligaments hold these bones together. Holding the steering wheel tightly or bracing against the dash for impact can transfer the energy of the crash through your stiffened arms to the wrist, elbow, and/or shoulder, where something may stretch, tear, or break. The shoulder is a "ball-and-socket" joint, similar to the hip.

As with any other joint, any part of the shoulder may be injured by trauma. The shoulder may be dislocated, strained, sprained, or a ligament may be stretched or torn.

Rotator Cuff Tear

A group of four major muscles and tendons comprise the rotator cuff (*subscapularis*, *supraspinatus*, *intraspinatus* and *teres minor*). It is the combination of these muscles and tendons which create a capsule surrounding the three main bones (*humerus*, *clavicle*, and *scapula*) that comprise the rotator cuff. The rotator cuff

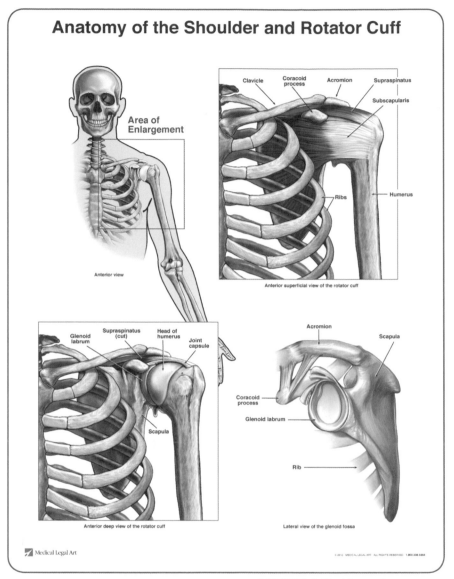

Anatomy of the Shoulder and Rotator Cuff

Area of Enlargement

Anterior view

Clavicle | Coracoid process | Acromion | Supraspinatus

Subscapularis

Ribs | Humerus

Anterior superficial view of the rotator cuff

Glenoid labrum | Supraspinatus (cut) | Head of humerus | Joint capsule

Scapula

Anterior deep view of the rotator cuff

Acromion | Scapula

Coracoid process

Glenoid labrum

Rib

Lateral view of the glenoid fossa

Medical Legal Art

© 2010 MEDICAL LEGAL ART ALL RIGHTS RESERVED 1.800.338.5954

©1997-2010 Medical Legal Art. www.doereport.com

surrounds the shoulder joint and connects the rotator cuff muscles to the upper arm bone. *Tendons* of the *rotator cuff* can be partially or completely torn by trauma.

These muscles and tendons hold the humerus in the shoulder socket and allow for the shoulder to move with the greatest range of motion of any joint in the human body.

A traumatic injury to the shoulder capsule occurs when the tendons or muscles get torn. These traumatic tears can be either partial or complete (fully through the tissue). The symptoms of this injury may include pain upon movement of the shoulder, pain with arm exertion, pain when lying on the side of the damaged shoulder, and/or loss of strength of the affected arm. More severe rotator cuff tears will cause constant aching and pain.

A traumatic tear of the rotator cuff likely results from acceleration-deceleration and rotational forces applied through the arm to the shoulder joint structures. This can occur in a number of ways, such as when the occupant of a car is holding on to the wheel bracing for an impact, or when a pedestrian or cyclist falls and uses their arm(s) to lessen the impact of the fall.

Impingement Syndrome

Shoulder impingement may occur when the rotator cuff muscles are injured. The muscles may begin to swell, which puts pressure on the small blood vessels supplying the muscle. With decreased blood flow, the muscle fibers begin to weaken and fray, like the strands of a rope. A rotator cuff injury is often accompanied by impingement syndrome. Disruption of the joint structures and edema (swelling) can cause the rotator cuff tendons to rub against the acromion causing painful symptoms. Sometimes an individual can have a shoulder joint that is degenerating from age or wear and tear, but not have any pain or limitations. This asymptomatic impingement syndrome can become symptomatic following trauma to the shoulder.

Acromioclavicular (AC) Injury

The point that we touch on top of the shoulder is the *acromion*, and it is one part of the shoulder blade (the scapula). The collarbone (called the *clavicular*) meets the acromion at the acromioclavicular (AC) joint. The AC joint is the only point of bone attachment of the upper limb to the rest of the skeleton. This joint can be traumatically injured resulting in an acromioclavicular joint separation.

An AC separation is not the same as a shoulder dislocation. In a shoulder dislocation, the humerus is displaced from the socket of the joint. An AC separation is a disruption of the joint between the clavicle and the scapula. This injury nearly always results from a sudden trauma, such as a direct blow, falling on an outstretched hand, or having your arm on the dashboard as you braced yourself for impact.

Symptoms of an AC separation include pain, usually severe at the time of the initial injury, and swelling. A visible bump caused by the separated joint may be apparent in a severe AC separation.

Treatment

Rotator cuff tears and impingement syndrome are often first treated conservatively (physical therapy, chiropractic, massage therapy, acupuncture), with the intent being to decrease inflammation, return mobility to the joint, and strengthen the supporting muscle structures. Pain that persists after conservative treatment may indicate the need for orthopedic surgery to address the tear and/or impingement syndrome.

Shoulder surgery is usually accompanied with arthroscopy, where the surgeon can view the joint with a camera through small incisions. If there is impingement of the tendons, the surgeon may do an *acromioplasty*. This surgical procedure *decompresses* or takes the pressure off the rotator cuff by shaping or removing bone spurs that developed or were worsened by trauma in order to increase space between the tendons and the surface of the acromion. This should result in decreased pain and increase motion in the joint.

If the tendon is torn, it may be repaired through an arthoscopic procedure, or may sometimes require a larger incision to better perform the necessary repair. The repair consists of stitching together the tear or reattaching the tendon to the bone.

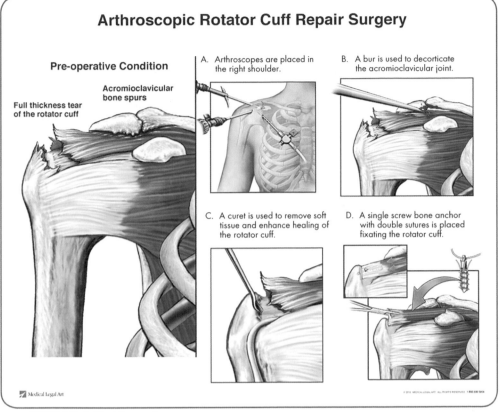

Arthroscopic Rotator Cuff Repair Surgery

Pre-operative Condition

Full thickness tear
of the rotator cuff

Acromioclavicular
bone spurs

A. Arthroscopes are placed in the right shoulder.

B. A bur is used to decorticate the acromioclavicular joint.

C. A curet is used to remove soft tissue and enhance healing of the rotator cuff.

D. A single screw bone anchor with double sutures is placed fixating the rotator cuff.

Medical Legal Art

Depending upon the patient, the extent of injuries, and the amount of surgical repair necessary, the post-surgery healing time can be from sixty days to six months or more. Regardless of post-surgery healing time, recuperation from this kind of surgery is an inconvenient process. Post-surgery rehabilitation most often includes motion therapies to return mobility and strength to the repaired shoulder.

BRAIN AND HEAD INJURIES
CHAPTER 39

A. How the Brain Gets Injured

The brain can be injured in a variety of ways. We will look at three ways in particular:

> skull fracture or skull penetration;
>
> acceleration-deceleration injuries; and
>
> coup/contre-coup injuries.

1. Skull Fracture

Let's start with a basic understanding of the skull and traumatic brain injury. Brain injury can occur when the skull is fractured, resulting in brain swelling, brain contusion (bruise), or an entry point for bacteria and infection. Brain injury can also occur without a skull fracture, such as "shaken baby syndrome," or when a bicycle rider's head hits the windshield of a car or pavement, or when an occupant of a car is rear-ended and sufficient crash forces are transmitted through the car. The skull is a very strong structure made by strong bones fused together. The inside of the skull is not a smooth surface, but bumpy with ridges. It takes significant force to break or crack the skull. The brain, on the other hand, is a very soft, gelatin-like tissue

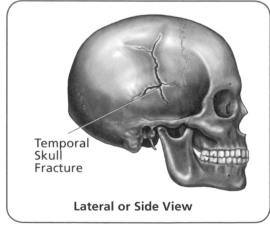

Temporal Skull Fracture

Lateral or Side View

Illustration ©2010 Nucleus Medical Media. All rights reserved. www.nucleusinc.com

RICHARD H. ADLER
Attorney at Law, Adler Giersch PS

structure similar to Jell-O. A force that passes through the skull and penetrates the brain may cause severe injury. The skull is thinnest, and therefore the weakest, at the temporal lobe, which is near the ear. As a result, many skull fractures occur in the area of the temporal lobe.

2. Acceleration-Deceleration Injuries

The key to understanding the role of acceleration-deceleration forces in causing traumatic brain injury is inertia. This means that an object remains stationary or in motion until acted upon by some outside force. In traumatic brain injury, the brain has inertia. For example, when a person falls backwards onto a hard floor, the back of the person's head hits the floor and stops. The brain, however, is still moving until it strikes the inside of the skull. If the brain gets bruised, there is bleeding, also called a hemorrhage. This bleeding causes further damage to the brain.

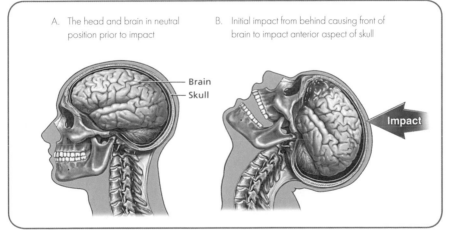

A. The head and brain in neutral position prior to impact

B. Initial impact from behind causing front of brain to impact anterior aspect of skull

Brain
Skull

Impact

The skull does not have to strike an object in order for the brain to get injured. There are many situations in motor vehicle crashes where the forces are transmitted through the brain without the skull hitting the dashboard, windshield, steering wheel, or window.

Let's look at acceleration-deceleration injuries in a rear-end motor vehicle collision. When a car is rear-ended, there is a certain amount of force transmitted through the car. As a result, the occupants of the car begin to move forward. The brain, inside the skull, floats in a bath of cerebral spinal fluid and remains stationary due to the membranes of the brain that attach to the skull. When the neck reaches the end point of moving forward, the head may suddenly stop, while the brain continues forward slamming into the interior structure of the skull. Contusions of the brain are usually more severe in parts of the brain closest to skull, including the tips of the frontal and temporal lobes. The undersurface of these lobes is quite vulnerable because they are located next to skull structures that are rough and irregular. And side to side motion of the brain, caused by a side-impact, can bruise or tear these tissues.

3. Coup/Contre-Coup Injuries

Related to acceleration-deceleration injuries, are *coup/contre-coup* injuries. These happen with a severe impact or after a fall when the head is struck. After the brain hits the inside of the skull, it might actually bounce back and strike the opposite side of the skull, potentially resulting in two separate injuries to the brain.

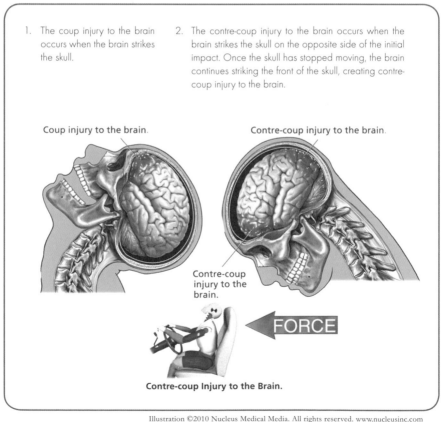

1. The coup injury to the brain occurs when the brain strikes the skull.

2. The contre-coup injury to the brain occurs when the brain strikes the skull on the opposite side of the initial impact. Once the skull has stopped moving, the brain continues striking the front of the skull, creating contre-coup injury to the brain.

Coup injury to the brain.

Contre-coup injury to the brain.

Contre-coup injury to the brain.

FORCE

Contre-coup Injury to the Brain.

Illustration ©2010 Nucleus Medical Media. All rights reserved. www.nucleusinc.com

RICHARD H. ADLER
Attorney at Law, Adler Giersch PS

B. Types of Brain Injury

We now have a sense of how the brain gets injured. Let's review what happens to brain cells in traumatic brain injury.

1. Contusion of the Brain

Contusion (bruise) of the brain's surface occurs when the brain strikes the bone within the skull. Contusions occur at the tips of the brain: frontal (front), temporal (side), and occipital (rear). Large contusions may be seen on CT scans or MRIs as large bruises. Areas of visible contusion are surrounded by a zone of swelling, known as "edema." If this swelling is great enough, it may cause changes in consciousness, and in severe cases, may be life threatening. However, contusions are often microscopic hemorrhages too small to be seen on currently used CT or MRI imaging tests. There is hope that in the near future technological advances with CT and MRI tests will allow better visualization of these hemorrhages.

2. Diffuse Axonal Injury

We mentioned previously that the whole brain is a gelatin-like structure. However, each part of the brain has a different consistency and density. For instance, gray matter, which are the nerve cells, and white matter, the long connecting "tails," or axons, of the nerves have different weights. With trau-

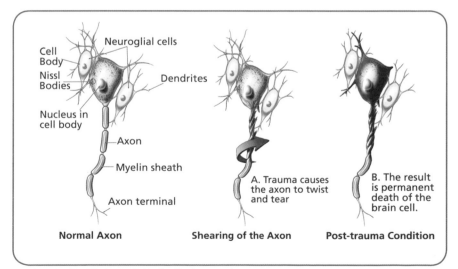

matic brain injury, the brain undergoes a rapid deformation. When the brain is rapidly moved, different parts move at different speeds. This can cause nerves to be stretched or torn within the brain. This type of injury is often known as a shearing (stretched and torn) injury or "diffuse axonal injury," since the nerve fibers are sheared at the margin of the gray and white matter. A diffuse axonal injury can occur without a skull fracture or brain contusion. This stretching of the axon can kill the cell and destroy its connection to other cells. Torn axons cannot be repaired.

Diffuse axonal injuries are often very difficult to diagnose because CT scans and MRIs may not be able to detect the microscopic lesions that occur from these types of injuries. Unfortunately, diffuse axonal injuries may result in prolonged or permanent behavioral, cognitive and overall disability.

3. Excito-toxic Injuries

Following a traumatic brain injury, damaged cells or neurons will release an excessive amount of the chemicals that are

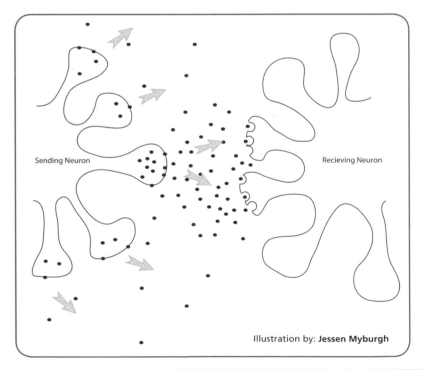

Sending Neuron

Recieving Neuron

Illustration by: **Jessen Myburgh**

used to transmit messages, called "neurotransmitters." When neurons are damaged, they may release such large amounts of chemicals, such as Glutamate and Aspartate, that they damage the next neuron. These chemicals, in turn, stimulate neighboring neurons, causing a chain of events that will lead to eventual death of those cells. This is known as an excito-toxic effect. These types of injuries may not be seen immediately but can develop over several days following the initial head trauma. This delayed chemical process may help to explain the delayed onset of symptoms experienced by some survivors of traumatic brain injury.

C. **Brain Anatomy**

Scientists, doctors, attorneys, poets, and artists describe the brain in many ways. This organ controls thinking, sight, taste, touch, sound, and smell. It is also the area of our body that controls judgment, emotions, and the ability to distinguish between pleasant and unpleasant. Additionally, the brain controls motor functions (muscles), sleep, and our autonomic functions, such as heart rate.

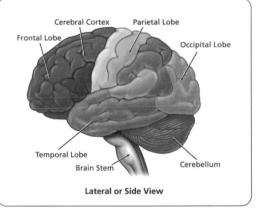

The brain has the make-up or texture of a sponge or gelatin. Some doctors referred to the brain's texture as Jell-O like. It weighs about three pounds.

The brain has many important parts, which I will briefly discuss:

1. Cerebral Cortex (also called the Cerebrum);
2. Cerebellum;
3. Brain Stem;
4. Membranes and Cerebrospinal Fluid;
5. Skull.

The Cerebral Cortex, Cerebellum, and the Brain Stem comprise approximately 80 percent of the contents of the skull, with the remaining 20 percent consisting of Membranes and Cerebrospinal fluids. Although the skull is not technically a part of the brain, it is an important structure to understand. While its role is to protect the brain from outside forces, it can also contribute to brain tissue damage because of sharp ridges on the inside in places just below the forehead.

1. Cerebral Cortex or Cerebrum

The largest part of the brain is the cerebral cortex, also known as the Cerebrum. This structure is divided into two halves (or hemispheres) but connected by a bridge-like structure called the Corpus Callosum.

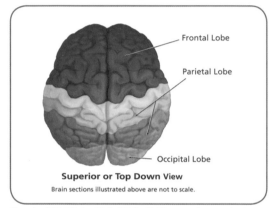

Frontal Lobe

Parietal Lobe

Occipital Lobe

Superior or Top Down View

Brain sections illustrated above are not to scale.

These two hemispheres control speech, memory, and intelligence. The right hemisphere controls movement on the left side of the body and the left hemisphere controls movement on the right side. The Corpus Callosum carries nerve fibers from one side to the other, and therefore carries messages between the two cerebral hemispheres.

a. Lobes of the Cerebral Cortex

The two cerebral hemispheres are further divided into various sections. There are four sections in each hemisphere, called lobes. Each lobe plays a critical function, and all work together as an integrated system.

i. The Frontal Lobe

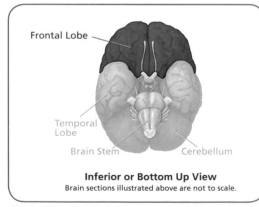

Frontal Lobe

Temporal Lobe

Brain Stem

Cerebellum

Inferior or Bottom Up View

Brain sections illustrated above are not to scale.

Located just behind the skull of the forehead, the frontal lobe governs our ability to reason, make judgments, organize and integrate information, and control some motor/

muscle functions. It also holds the key to our personality and moods. It is easy to see why this lobe has come to be known as the area that manages our "executive functions." An injury to this area can have a significant and

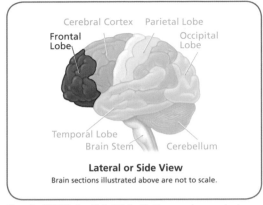

negative effect on many activities in the life of a traumatic brain injury (TBI) survivor because it compromises the ability to organize time, projects, and tasks. The location of the frontal lobe makes it more susceptible to injury in situations where one hits their head on a windshield, dashboard, or steering wheel in a motor vehicle collision. Moreover, even in cases where the head does not hit a solid object, the frontal lobes may be injured by colliding with the bony ridges of the skull behind the eyes.

ii. The Parietal Lobe

Located directly behind the frontal lobe, the parietal lobe provides and identifies sensory information such as touch, heat, cold, and pressure, and distinguishes objects and sounds. It also provides naming, reading, writing, and mathematical problem-solving functions. Another function of the parietal lobe is to help analyze visual information in 3-D space.

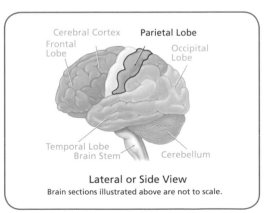

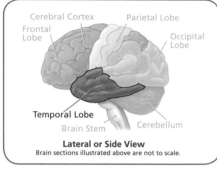

Illustration ©2010 Nucleus Medical Media.
All rights reserved. www.nucleusinc.com

iii.   The Temporal Lobe

The temporal lobe is located just above the ear and alongside both the frontal and parietal lobes. This part of the brain is related to hearing, smell, taste, and language comprehension.   Recognition of tone, pitch, and music is also processed here. The temporal and frontal lobes focus on short-term memory and processing new information. These lobes are the most frequently injured lobes of the brain.

iv. The Occipital Lobe

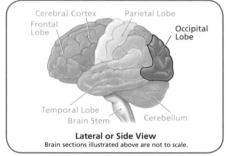

Illustration ©2010 Nucleus Medical Media.
All rights reserved. www.nucleusinc.com

Located at the back of the skull, the occipital lobe is involved primarily with vision. This lobe gives and receives impulses to interpret objects and store information related to vision. Injuries to the occipital lobe can impact a person's ability to interpret spatial relationships, color perception, and other aspects of vision.

2. Cerebellum

Towards the back of the Cerebral Cortex and beneath the Occipital Lobes lies the Cerebellum. The Cerebellum has two hemispheres just like the Cerebral Cortex, with a mid-line bridge connecting both hemispheres. The Cerebellum coordinates many functions involving balance,

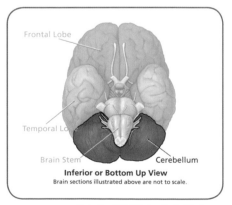

Illustration ©2010 Nucleus Medical Media.
All rights reserved. www.nucleusinc.com

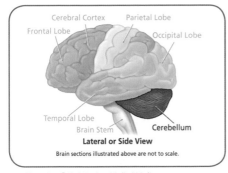

Lateral or Side View
Brain sections illustrated above are not to scale.

posture, and equilibrium. The Cerebellum also regulates many automatic responses such as voluntary muscle movement. It operates "blueprints" of previously learned complex motor tasks, such as playing a musical instrument or doing a gymnastics routine.

3. The Brain Stem

Another major part of the brain, the Brain Stem, is located beneath the Cerebral Cortex but in front of the Cerebellum. Just as it sounds, this structure connects the brain to the spinal cord. It is through the brain stem that messages and

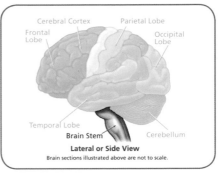

Lateral or Side View
Brain sections illustrated above are not to scale.

nerve impulses going from the brain to the rest of the body must travel. Most of the important functions of the body are centered in the Brain Stem, including respiration, blood pressure, circulation, and sleep cycle regulation. Additionally, twelve cranial nerves begin in the Brain Stem, responsible for activity such as smell, swallowing, hearing, vision, eye movement, facial sensation, taste, and muscle movements in the face, neck, shoulders,

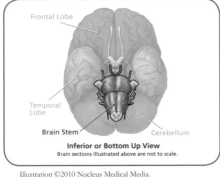

Inferior or Bottom Up View
Brain sections illustrated above are not to scale.

and tongue.

4. Membranes and Cerebrospinal Fluid

As mentioned above, 80 percent of the brain is made up of the Cerebral

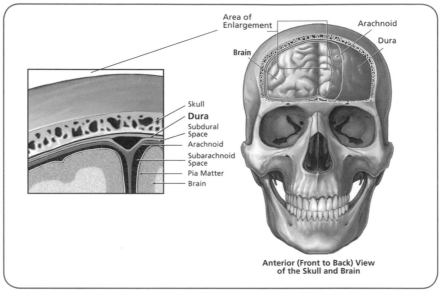

Cortex, Cerebellum and the Brain Stem. However, there is another 20 percent of the brain consisting of membranes and cerebrospinal fluid which plays a vital and critical role in all brain activity. There are three layers of membranes covering the brain, called the Dura, Arachnoid, and Pia Membranes. Membranes are also known as *Meninges*. These membranes appear thin and clear and have a role of supporting and protecting the brain as well as assisting and separating its different parts. An injury to the membrane may be very important in certain types of TBI.

a. Dura Mater Membrane

The outermost membrane just inside the skull is known as the Dura Mater or Dura. Very small blood vessels carrying nutrients to the brain travel through the Dura Mater. The veins in this blood supply have very thin walls. If the Dura is somehow disturbed during trauma, blood may escape into the space

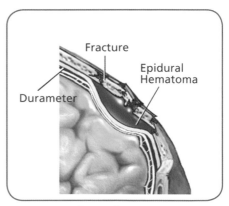

between the Dura and the skull, and rapidly enlarge and form a clot called a hematoma. These clots are named by their location, such as an epidural or subdural hematoma. An epidural hematoma refers to a blood clot that is located outside the Dura. A subdural hematoma means the blood

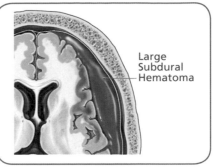

Large
Subdural
Hematoma

clot is located below the Dura. Blood clots of these types are very dangerous because they may distort and displace underlying brain tissue, compressing brain cells and the connecting tissues, and reducing blood flow. Because the brain is located in a closed space (the skull), a large blood clot that develops from bleeding blood vessels is a medical emergency, since there is no room to allow for expansion or swelling following traumatic brain injury. Depending upon their size and location, hematomas and blood clots have to be removed surgically.

b. Arachnoid Membrane

The second or the middle membrane is known as the Arachnoid Membrane. This middle membrane does not let any liquid pass

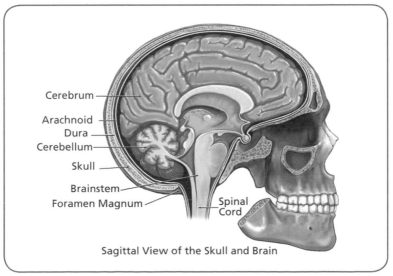

Cerebrum

Arachnoid
Dura
Cerebellum

Skull

Brainstem
Foramen Magnum

Spinal
Cord

Sagittal View of the Skull and Brain

through it. This allows for uniform distribution of the fluid throughout the brain.

c. Pia Membrane

The arachnoid membrane is separated from the third membrane, the pia membrane, by the subarachnoid space. This is where cerebrospinal fluid flows. Following traumatic brain injury, bleeding is possible in the subarachnoid space and may create a medical emergency.

d. Cerebrospinal Fluid

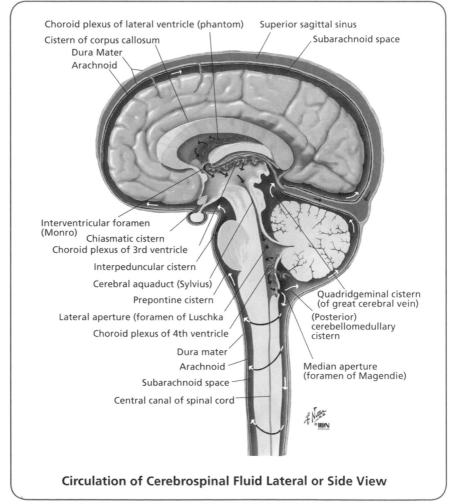

Choroid plexus of lateral ventricle (phantom)
Cistern of corpus callosum
Dura Mater
Arachnoid
Superior sagittal sinus
Subarachnoid space

Interventricular foramen (Monro)
Chiasmatic cistern
Choroid plexus of 3rd ventricle
Interpeduncular cistern
Cerebral aqueduct (Sylvius)
Prepontine cistern
Lateral aperture (foramen of Luschka
Choroid plexus of 4th ventricle
Dura mater
Arachnoid
Subarachnoid space
Central canal of spinal cord

Quadridgeminal cistern (of great cerebral vein)
(Posterior) cerebellomedullary cistern
Median aperture (foramen of Magendie)

Circulation of Cerebrospinal Fluid Lateral or Side View

Illustration ©2010 Nucleus Medical Media. All rights reserved. www.nucleusinc.com

Cerebrospinal fluid is a clear liquid and serves to buffer the three membranes from each other, but also acts as a buffer for the brain itself. The cerebrospinal fluid is critical because it carries nutrients between blood vessels and brain cells.

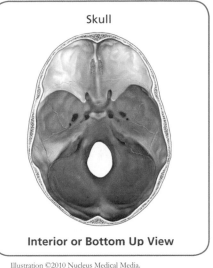

Skull

Interior or Bottom Up View

5. The Skull

The skull protects the brain from outside infections and the bumps of daily life. The skull feels smooth on the outside when you run your hand over your head or across your forehead. However, as you can see from the illustration on this page, it is a very different story on the inside. The skull's interior surface is not smooth. It is marked by sharp edges located very close to nerves, tissue, and blood vessels. When a brain collides with and rides over these bony structures during trauma, the potential for injury is easy to understand.

D. Facts About Concussion and Traumatic Brain Injury

The word "concussion" is frequently used to describe an event in which the head is struck or strikes something, such as when athletes talk about having their "bell rung." A concussion is a traumatic brain injury and all brain injuries are serious. As a result of increased understanding of brain injury, concussions are now taken more seriously by school districts, medical personnel, coaches, athletic trainers, parents, and student athletes.

E. Definitions of Mild Traumatic Brain Injury and its Symptoms

A great majority of traumatic brain injuries from a medical and legal standpoint are classified as "mild" TBIs. Unfortunately, this label somehow implies that the injury is minor or trivial. However, the word "mild" describes only the initial insult relative to the degree of neurological severity. The use of mild usually does not relate to the degree of short- or long-term functional difficulties or disability.

Mild Traumatic Brain Injury (MTBI) has been defined by the Mild Trauma Brain Injury Committee of the American Congress of Rehabilitation Medicine as follows:

> A patient with a mild traumatic brain injury is a person who has had a traumatically induced physiological disruption of brain function, as manifested by at least one of the following:
>
> #1. any period of loss of the consciousness;
>
> #2. any loss of memory for events immediately before or after the accident;
>
> #3. any alteration in mental state at the time of the accident (e.g., feeling dazed, disoriented or confused); and
>
> #4. focal neurological deficit(s) that may or not be transient; but where the severity of the injury does not exceed the following:
>
> > a) loss of consciousness of approximately 30 minutes or less;
> >
> > b) after 30 minutes an initial Glasgow Coma Scale of 13/15 (see page 178);
> >
> > c) post traumatic amnesia not greater than 24 hours.

There is a range of common symptoms that may result after traumatic brain injury.

Physical Problems

- headaches
- dizziness and balance difficulties
- fatigue
- visual changes
- loss of taste or smell
- sensitivity to light or noise

- sleep difficulties
- change in sex drive

Cognitive Problems

- memory loss
- disorientation
- lack of concentration
- distractability
- difficulty with decision-making
- difficulty with problem-solving
- difficulty with organizing tasks
- difficulty with doing more than one task at a time
- difficulty with math calculations
- difficulty with reading
- forgetfulness
- changes in speech pattern
- word retrieval difficulty
- inability to express onself

Emotional Problems

- easily irritated and angered
- frustration
- depression
- mood swings, such as feeling sad, anxious, or listless
- lack of motivation
- difficulty initiating and following through with activities

Most survivors of traumatic brain injury do not have every symptom, but often will have at least several from each category.

Most individuals who have sustained a mild TBI will recover well within the first one to nine months, especially those who do not also sustain secondary injuries such as musculoskeletal injury. There is a subset of individuals who have persistent problems after a mild TBI and report continuing problems with attention, memory, sleep changes, headaches and other pain symptoms, fatigue, and other post-concussion symptoms beyond the usual recovery time of one to nine months. Many of these individuals suffer depression, anxiety, and/or posttraumatic stress that complicate the recovery process.

F. Measuring Coma

A coma is a state of unconsciousness from which the person cannot be aroused, even by powerful stimulation. To measure the level of consciousness versus unconsciousness in acute or emergency care settings such as hospitals, the Glasgow Coma Scale (GCS) is often used. The Glasgow Coma Scale rates eye response, motor response (arm and legs), and verbal response.

Best Eye Opening (maximum of 4 points)

4 = Spontaneous – open with blinking at baseline

3 = To voice, command, speech

2 = To pain only

1 = No response

Best Motor Response (maximum of 6 points)

6 = Follows commands for movement

5 = Purposeful movement to pain

4 = Withdraws in response to pain

3 = Flexion in response to pain

2 = Extension in response to pain

1 = No response

Best Verbal Response (maximum of 5 points)

5 = Oriented and conversational

4 = Disoriented and confused conversation, but able to answer questions

3 = Inappropriate words

2 = Incomprehensible sounds or speech

1 = No response

The number from each category is then added together for a total score. This score is measured against a standard rating system.

INNER EAR —
DIZZINESS AND VERTIGO
CHAPTER 40

Dizziness or vertigo can result from a traumatic injury to the head, brain, neck, temporomandibular joint, or inner ear. An injury to the inner ear is also known as a *vestibular injury.*

This can result in loss of balance, nausea, and in severe situations, fully disrupt a person's life as it impacts their ability to drive, work, walk, etc. This injury affects the vestibular nerve, which carries balance signals from the inner ear to the brain. With an injury to the vestibular nerve, information signals to the brain regarding motion are not properly sent or

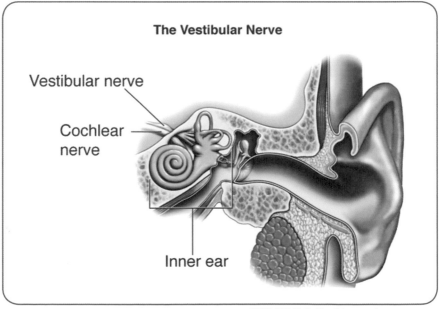

The Vestibular Nerve

Vestibular nerve

Cochlear nerve

Inner ear

©1997-2010 Medical Legal Art. www.doereport.com

RICHARD H. ADLER
Attorney at Law, Adler Giersch PS

received, resulting in the sensation of dizziness or vertigo.

The inner ear controls your balance. Within the inner ear there are crystals know as *otoconia*. When the inner ear is traumatized, crystals get dislodged and become free-floating within semicircular canals filled with a liquid-type substance known as *endolymph*. When the crystals are dislodged, they travel through the endolymph and come in contact with hair cells or nerve endings, called *cupula*. These nerve endings control a person's balance. When the free-floating crystals contact the hair cells, dizziness results.

An inner ear or a vestibular injury is frequently not diagnosed immediately after a traumatic injury, since several medical conditions can create symptoms of dizziness or vertigo, such as a neck injury or a reaction to medication. If a healthcare provider suspects a vestibular injury, he/she may refer you to an otolar-

> *Within the inner ear there are crystals know as otoconia. When the free-floating crystals contact the hair cells, dizziness results.*

yngologist, a specialist more commonly known as an ear, nose, and throat (or ENT) specialist.

If a vestibular injury is diagnosed, the specialist may recommend several different treatment approaches depending on the specifics and severity of the injury. An inner ear or vestibular type injury may resolve spontaneously over time, requiring only a "wait-and-see" approach. If the condition does not resolve spontaneously or has been present for some time, the doctor may recommend use of a steroid or non-steroidal medication.

Additionally, specific therapy known as vestibular rehabilitation is available. This treatment is similar to physical therapy for musculoskeletal injuries, but it focuses on treatment for inner ear dysfunction. If the injury is severe and disabling, surgery may ultimately be required.

The purpose of vestibular rehabilitation therapy is to reposition the crystals away from the nerve endings -- this is accomplished by rotating the body and head in a certain way, which moves them away from the nerve endings and relieves the sense of dizziness and vertigo. This treatment has proven effective for many people, but not all. Even when the treatment proves effective, it may not lead to a permanent cure. Your daily activities or even a cold or flu can result in the crystals moving again. Once these crystals have been dislodged by trauma, there may be ongoing recurrences. When this happens, there remains a high likelihood of reoccurrence for the remainder of your life. The movement of the loosened crystals can be triggered by upper respiratory infection, rapid head movement, working with the head in a certain position, driving a car, airplane travel, or recreational use of a boat due to the jarring of the boat on the water.

Recurring symptoms may be brief, lasting moments, or continue on for days and weeks. Further physical therapy, chiropractic care, acupuncture, massage therapy, or medications may be beneficial.

SCARS

Large and obvious scarring will be permanent. Many scars can be reduced and sometimes eliminated by a plastic surgeon. If you develop a scar following a traumatic injury or surgery, ask the treating doctor to refer you to a plastic surgeon for consultation.

This specialist will examine your scar and advise you whether any procedure(s) can improve the scarring, as well as informing you of the cost of such treatment.

Scars come in many sizes and shapes, and as a result, they are not easy to evaluate. Straight scars that have been brought together well with stitches will lessen, and six to twelve months later may be less noticeable. However, jagged or deep scars can result in contraction of muscles and may remain visible. The size and shape of a scar are just two factors to look at in case valuation, as is the location of the scar. A scar impairing the obvious physical appearance of a man or woman will have greater value than one that's often covered up by clothing. Also, a scar that may impact your work performance will influence the compensation of your case. For example, a facial scar on a sales representative will have a different impact to the case then a thigh scar on a construction worker.

> *The size and shape of a scar are just two factors to look at in case valuation, as is the location of the scar.*

POST-TRAUMATIC STRESS DISORDER (PTSD)

CHAPTER 42

Post-traumatic stress disorder (PTSD) is a diagnosis frequently made for patients who have survived a serious traumatic event, but it is also a diagnosis that is greatly misunderstood.

> *However, the mere presence of psychological distress related to traumatic injury does not necessarily mean the patient has post-traumatic stress disorder.*

There is no doubt that physical trauma caused by motor vehicle crashes, falls, burns, or loss of a limb can, and often does, result in significant pain and emotional trauma injury. However, the mere presence of psychological distress related to traumatic injury does not necessarily mean the patient has post-traumatic stress disorder.

In order for a psychological injury to rise to the level of a diagnosis of PTSD, it must meet all of the specific diagnostic criteria of the *DSM-IV (Diagnostic and Statistical Manual — 4th edition)* published by the American Psychological Association, including the following:

✳ **Exposure to a traumatic event** in which "the person experienced, witnessed, or was confronted with . . . actual or threatened death or serious injury, or a threat to the physical integrity of self or others." The patient must also have experienced the event with "intense fear, helplessness, or horror."

✳ **The traumatic event is persistently re-experienced** "by distressing recollections of the event, distressing dreams,

RICHARD H. ADLER
Attorney at Law, Adler Giersch PS

reliving of the event, or intense psychological or physical distress at exposure to cues that remind the patient of the trauma."

✳ **Persistent avoidance of stimuli associated with the trauma** or "numbing" of the senses. Examples include: avoiding thoughts of the event; avoiding activities, places, or people that arouse memories of the event; inability to recall important aspects of the trauma; diminished interest or participation in life activities; feelings of detachment; reduced range of emotional expression; or a lack of a sense of future.

✳ **Persistent symptoms of increased arousal.** Examples are: insomnia, irritability, difficulty concentrating, or an exaggerated startle response.

✳ **A duration of more than one month**, with a disturbance in the person's social and work life.

Clearly, the diagnosis of PTSD is detailed and specific. Oftentimes, when PTSD is suspected, the actual psychological dysfunction may be of a lesser nature, commonly diagnosed as "stress disorder" or "phobic reaction."

In the area of motor vehicle crashes, there are characteristics that make for a greater risk of PTSD or related psychological symptoms, including:

1. **The event is completely out of the individual's control**, much like an unprovoked and completely unexpected physical attack.

2. **The event causing the traumatic injury** involves feelings of helplessness and fear; the victim was unable to do anything to avoid or prevent it.

3. **Phobias.** Fear of driving or fear of the traumatic event's location.

4. **Injuries can be very painful**. PTSD has been associated not only with the physical trauma of a violent event, but also arising from intense pain experienced by the patient separate from the traumatic event itself. Prolonged and severe pain experienced immediately after a traumatic injury, but before

the intervention of care, can be the traumatic experience itself leading to PTSD symptoms.

©cultura Photography/Veer

5. **Cognitive disorders can increase symptoms**. Cognitive disorders following trauma are often not diagnosed early on. This can have a very negative psychological impact on those who experience further fear, anxiety, or depression because real symptoms are not believed or validated by the treatment provider. This can lead to the exacerbation of PTSD symptoms.

Treatment and therapy for PTSD will most likely include "desensitizing" techniques. In the case of those with a new fear of driving, travel, or the location of the trauma, therapy will likely include repeated exposure to the phobic stimuli, including "imagining" the traumatic event. These techniques result in desensitizing the patient to the impact of the event, thereby lessening or eliminating the victim's fear. Cognitive behavior therapy and relaxation training used in the treatment of chronic pain have also been effective in the treatment of PTSD symptoms. In certain situations, medications, including antidepressant drugs, are needed.

If you experience depression, anxiety or other symptoms of psychological stress following a traumatic injury, it is important to talk with your doctor or healthcare providers so that the condition can be assessed and, if needed, referred to an appropriate specialist for evaluation or treatment.

Not surprisingly, PTSD may be denied or contested by insurers, as it is traditionally considered a purely psychological disorder. In fact, until recently, PTSD without a related physical injury was excluded from coverage under UM/UIM policies.

That changed with a precedent-setting decision from the State of Washington Court of Appeals in *Trinh v. Allstate Insurance.*[1] ADLER ◆ GIERSCH PS represented Lien Trinh for injuries sustained in a collision involving an uninsured driver. In that case, Ms. Trinh had a flat tire on Interstate 5 and called a friend, Pete Drosdal, to help. While changing the tire, Mr. Drosdal was struck and killed by an uninsured drunk driver. Ms. Trinh was standing next to Mr. Drosdal when he was struck, but she was not hit.

Though not physically injured, Ms. Trinh was diagnosed with Post-Traumatic Stress Disorder as a result of witnessing the traumatic death of her friend and good samaritan. This condition was accompanied by physical symptoms including headaches, nausea and vomiting, hair loss, chronic crying, insomnia, and depression. Allstate Insurance Company denied coverage under Ms. Trinh's Uninsured Motorist policy, finding that Ms. Trinh's Post-Traumatic Stress Disorder was not a "bodily injury" as defined by her insurance contract.

We filed a lawsuit on behalf of Ms. Trinh against Allstate in King County Superior Court, seeking a judgment that Ms. Trinh's condition was covered under the Uninsured Motorist policy. Allstate countered, and the trial judge agreed with Allstate and dismissed Ms. Trinh's claim. Ms. Trinh appealed the decision to the Washington State Court of Appeals. On January 14, 2002, the Court issued an opinion in favor of Ms. Trinh, reversing the trial court's dismissal. Allstate then appealed the decision to the Washington State Supreme Court, who declined to review the case. As a result, the Court of Appeals decision stands as the law in Washington and expands the understanding and recognition of the physical-injury nature of Post-Traumatic Stress Disorder in Washington State.

---

1   1 Trinh v Allstate, 37 P.3d 1259 (Washington Court Appeals, Division I, 2002)

TEMPOROMANDIBULAR JOINT (TMJ)

CHAPTER 43

Jaw problems are a common complaint following a motor vehicle collision. The joint between your upper and lower jaw is called the *temporomandibular joint* (TMJ). A TMJ injury can result from direct trauma to the mandible (lower jaw bone) or from a *hyperextension/hyperflexion* injury to the cervical spine without direct trauma to the mandible.

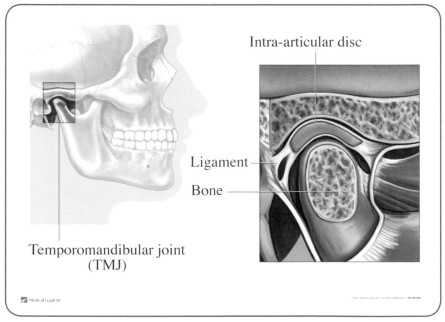

Intra-articular disc

Ligament

Bone

Temporomandibular joint
(TMJ)

Medical Legal Art

©1997-2010 Medical Legal Art. www.doereport.com

Your insurance company and the at-fault party's insurance company will likely not contest a jaw injury stemming from direct impact to the jaw. However, if a jaw injury results from a neck injury without a direct impact to the jaw, insurers often contest the relationship of the traumatic injury to the crash.

You should know that there are many studies that show a relationship to a TMJ injury, even when there has been no direct impact to the jaw.

For example, a study by Ralph Garcia, Jr., DDS, and John Arrington, MD, published in the *Journal of Cranial Mandibular Practice*, analyzed the relationship between neck injuries and TMJ injuries. Eighty-seven patients from motor vehicle collisions with neck pain and (1) TMJ symptoms; (2) but no direct trauma to the face, head, or mandible; and (3) no prior TMJ complaints, underwent magnetic resonance imaging (MRI) testing.[1] Since the study involved 87 patients, a total of 174 jaw joints (87 x 2) were imaged with MRI. Ten joints were eliminated from the study because of poor film quality, inability to visualize the disk, or inability of the patient to close their mouth properly due to pain. The results of the MRIs indicated the following:

> Improper movement was present in a vast majority of joints and only 13 percent of TMJs were found to be normal. Additionally, abnormal joint fluid and swelling was present in a majority of the TMJs.

The authors of this study stated:

> The fact that previously asymptomatic patients became symptomatic after a post MVA cervical whiplash injury supports the position that TMJ symptoms are reasonably related to cervical whiplash injury.

The authors came to several other conclusions:

1. Joint fluid (effusion or inflammation/edema) was extremely common (65 percent to 83 percent) in the motor vehicle collision patients in their study and extremely rare in asymptomatic/normal subjects (2 percent).

---

1   Garcia, R, and Arrington, J.A., *The Relationship Between Cervical Whiplash and Temporomandibular Joint Injuries: An MRI Study*, J Cranial Mandibular Prac, Vol. 14, No.3, 1996, pp. 223-239

2. Internal derangement of the TMJ was significantly more prevalent in the motor vehicle collision patients in their study than in asymptomatic/normal subjects.

3. Total TMJ abnormalities were much more prevalent in their motor vehicle collision patients than in asymptomatic/normal subjects.

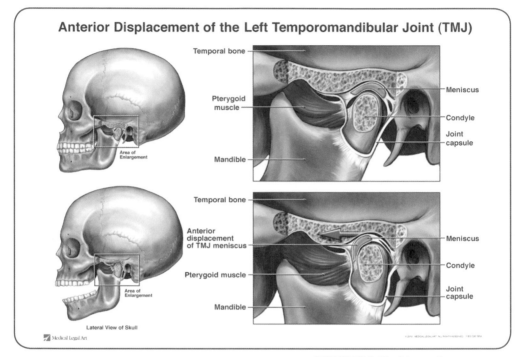

Anterior Displacement of the Left Temporomandibular Joint (TMJ)

©1997-2010 Medical Legal Art. www.doereport.com

Despite the findings in this study and many other research papers, your own automobile insurance company and the at-fault party's insurance company will often challenge whether your TMJ pain and symptoms could be caused by a motor vehicle crash, particularly if the jaw was not directly impacted. Legal consultation is advised early on so that appropriate evidence of injury can be preserved and noted. Remember, the more time that has elapsed between your injuries and treatment, the more room is created for an insurer to deny your claim by asserting that the injury and the traumatic event are not related. And a delay in obtaining appropriate evaluation and treatment may slow down your ultimate healthcare recovery.

THORACIC OUTLET SYNDROME (TOS)

CHAPTER 44

Another condition that arises after a traumatic spinal injury is *Thoracic Outlet Syndrome* (TOS), a condition associated with symptoms of arm pain, tingling or numbness, headache, neck pain, shoulder pain, chest pain, arm weakness, or hand weakness. Muscles in the front of the neck, called the *scalenes*, and the first rib form a triangular opening called the thoracic outlet.

TOS results from a closing of the space and compression of nerves and blood vessels (brachial plexus) which pass through an opening under the collarbone.

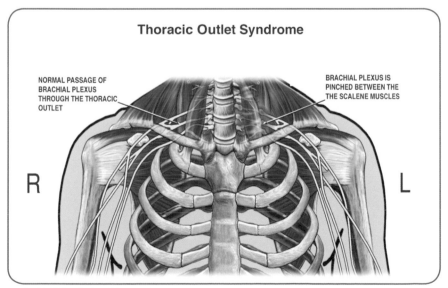

Thoracic Outlet Syndrome

NORMAL PASSAGE OF
BRACHIAL PLEXUS
THROUGH THE THORACIC
OUTLET

BRACHIAL PLEXUS IS
PINCHED BETWEEN THE
THE SCALENE MUSCLES

R

L

©1997-2010 Medical Legal Art. www.doereport.com

Chronic contraction of the scalene muscles narrows the thoracic outlet. The blood vessels and/or nerve structures of the brachial plexus are compressed, leading to the symptom patterns noted above. Arriving at a TOS diagnosis may be difficult because the condition takes time to develop and, once the symptoms are present, they can mimic other more common trauma-related conditions of the neck and/or shoulder.

If your symptoms resolve after the muscle block, then the doctor has established a cause-and-effect link between the scalene muscle tissue and your arm symptoms, confirming TOS.

It is common for a person with TOS, months after the trauma, to report symptoms of numbness and/or tingling in the arms, hands, and fingers, especially when the arm(s) are in an overhead position. This is because it takes time for the muscles and other injured structures to reduce the opening of the thoracic outlet. You might first notice the symptoms of TOS when your arms are in an elevated or up position such as when driving, washing or brushing your hair, or washing windows.

The vast majority of TOS cases primarily involve only nerve compression, with little or no vascular (blood flow) compromise. As a result, procedures and tests to evaluate vascular compression often find nothing abnormal. It is critical to have a thorough examination by a physician who is familiar with the condition, such as a vascular surgeon.

Establishing the cause of TOS from a traumatic injury usually requires careful examination of treatment records over time to identify symptoms and findings consistent with the diagnosis.

A common misconception in the insurance community (and often used as their argument to deny or deflate the value of a case) is that electrodiagnostic testing such as electromyelogram (EMG) and nerve conduction tests, can be relied on to confirm or rule out all types of TOS. However, these studies test the function of the compressed nerves and are not bulletproof. Negative results of an EMG and nerve studies do not rule out the TOS condition known as *neurogenic TOS*.

Insurance companies and their hired-gun physicians often challenge the validity of the TOS diagnosis in the absence of positive EMG testing or because the diagnosis relies primarily on the history provided by the patient and the clinical examination performed by the physician, rather than an objective test.

Vascular surgeons now often administer a *scalene muscle block*, an injection to the scalene muscle, to assist in diagnosing TOS. If your symptoms resolve after the muscle block, then the doctor has established a cause-and-effect link between the scalene muscle tissue and your arm symptoms, confirming TOS.

Initial treatment for TOS can be performed by physical therapists, chiropractors, acupuncturists, and/or licensed massage practitioners. The treatment is focused on stretching and relaxing the scalene muscles to allow the blood vessels and nerve structures to function unimpaired. Such treatment has been successful in treating TOS. When conservative modalities are not successful, surgery may be necessary to release the brachial plexus, typically by removing scalene muscle and part of the first rib to open up the outlet for the nerve and blood vessels.

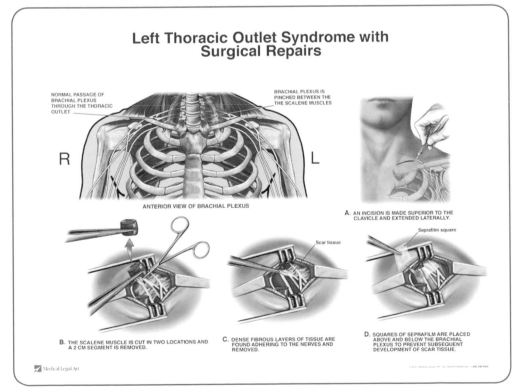

Left Thoracic Outlet Syndrome with Surgical Repairs

NORMAL PASSAGE OF BRACHIAL PLEXUS THROUGH THE THORACIC OUTLET

BRACHIAL PLEXUS IS PINCHED BETWEEN THE THE SCALENE MUSCLES

R   L

ANTERIOR VIEW OF BRACHIAL PLEXUS

A. AN INCISION IS MADE SUPERIOR TO THE CLAVICLE AND EXTENDED LATERALLY.

Scar tissue

Seprafilm square

B. THE SCALENE MUSCLE IS CUT IN TWO LOCATIONS AND A 2 CM SEGMENT IS REMOVED.

C. DENSE FIBROUS LAYERS OF TISSUE ARE FOUND ADHERING TO THE NERVES AND REMOVED.

D. SQUARES OF SEPRAFILM ARE PLACED ABOVE AND BELOW THE BRACHIAL PLEXUS TO PREVENT SUBSEQUENT DEVELOPMENT OF SCAR TISSUE.

Medical Legal Art

©1997-2010 Medical Legal Art. www.doereport.com

Carpal Tunnel
Syndrome (CTS)

CHAPTER 45

Carpal Tunnel Syndrome (CTS) occurs when tendons or ligaments in the wrist become enlarged from inflammation, often following a traumatic event like a car collision or repetitive use of the hands and arms.

The carpal "tunnel" is formed by a semi-circle of carpal bones on three sides and the transverse carpal ligament on the fourth side. The ligament is not designed to stretch or enlarge – there is only limited room in that opening. Through that opening passes the median nerve, nine tendons, and spongy tissue around the tendons called tenosynovium. When inflammation of these tendons and ligaments occurs, it pinches or compresses the median nerve, resulting in numbness or a tingling sensation to the fingers and muscles at the base of the thumb. In severe

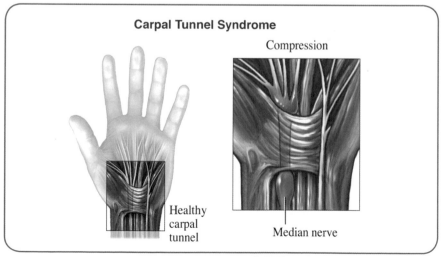

Carpal Tunnel Syndrome

Compression

Healthy carpal tunnel

Median nerve

©1997-2010 Medical Legal Art. www.doereport.com

situations this can be quite painful and result in weakness and loss of strength so that you cannot even write, keyboard, or lift a cup of coffee.

A driver in a motor vehicle collision can have a carpal tunnel injury when impacted either from behind or head-on. Such *acceleration/deceleration* forces can cause rapid and forceful *hyperextension* of the wrist when gripping the steering wheel.

Passengers in a car or others may also sustain a carpal tunnel injury when their hand(s) forcefully impacts another object, such as when bracing their hands on a dashboard. This stretches and stresses the structures within the carpal tunnel and inflammation or direct injuries to the nerve can result.

Symptoms of CTS may include periodic or constant numbness in one or both hands. You may complain of numbness of the entire hand, even though median neuropathy at the carpal tunnel affects only the thumb, index, and middle fingers. Symptoms may also include burning and/or tingling or numbness in the fingers, especially within the thumb, index, and middle fingers.

Numbness causes decreased dexterity, which may make it difficult to form a fist, grasp small objects (causing you to drop items), or perform other manual tasks.

Numbness may occur during a number of different activities including driving, writing, typing, sewing, or holding a book, magazine or newspaper. You may first experience symptoms at night when the affected hand is at rest and the body tries to pump-away the accumulation of fluid in the wrist and hand tissues.

Treatment for CTS may include workplace training to improve hand and work postures, or workplace ergonomic changes, which may reduce aggravation of the traumatically injured nerve. Other treatments include chiropractic adjustments, physical therapy, massage therapy, wrist splints to reduce the compression of the carpal tunnel by reducing motion of the wrist, and anti-inflammatory medications to reduce the inflammation within the carpal tunnel. When these measures fail, surgery of the carpal tunnel may be recommended to eliminate pressure upon the

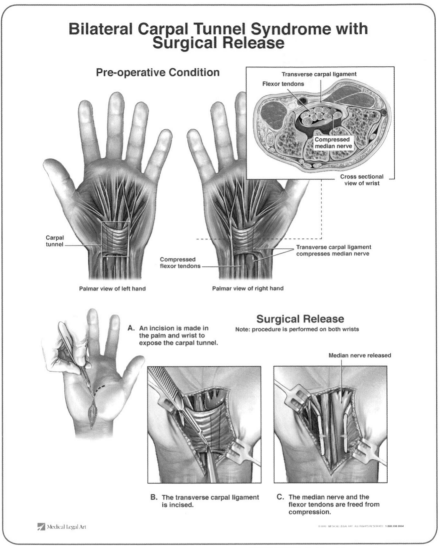

Bilateral Carpal Tunnel Syndrome with Surgical Release

Pre-operative Condition

Transverse carpal ligament

Flexor tendons

Compressed median nerve

Cross sectional view of wrist

Carpal tunnel

Compressed flexor tendons

Transverse carpal ligament compresses median nerve

Palmar view of left hand

Palmar view of right hand

Surgical Release

Note: procedure is performed on both wrists

A. An incision is made in the palm and wrist to expose the carpal tunnel.

Median nerve released

B. The transverse carpal ligament is incised.

C. The median nerve and the flexor tendons are freed from compression.

Medical Legal Art

©1997-2010 Medical Legal Art. www.doereport.com

median nerve. Failure to address traumatically induced CTS may result in permanent nerve damage. In untreated CTS cases, the muscles at the base of the thumb may even waste away.

Often the diagnosis of traumatic CTS is delayed because symptoms do not develop for weeks or months post-collision and the emergency room record does not indicate a hand injury.[1] One study suggests

1   Haas DC, Nord SQ, Bome MP; "Carpal Tunnel Syndrome Following Automobile Collisions."

CTS injuries may occur in as many as 22 percent of car collisions with reported injuries.[2] Diagnosis of a CTS injury may be further complicated by injury to other nerves in the same area, such as the *ulnar nerve* at the elbow.[3]

> Because of the delay in onset of symptoms and delay in diagnosis of CTS following a traumatic injury, its relationship to the trauma is often mistakenly attributed to work or lifestyle activities that involve repetitive hand or arm stress. An insurer often tries to deny a CTS injury by blaming non-traumatic causes.

It is important that you are clear with your doctor about the timing of the onset of symptoms, your lack of prior similar symptoms, and the mechanics of any traumatic injury.

Arch Phys Med Rehab 1981; 62:204-206.

2   Coert JH, Dellon AL; "Peripheral Nerve Entrapment Caused by Motor Vehicle Crashes." *J Trauma* 1994; 37: 1991-194

3   *Ibid* at 193

FIBROMYALGIA

CHAPTER 46

Well after the initial diagnosis of a musculoskeletal injury, some people develop chronic, widespread pain. While this could be caused by any number of injuries or factors, a small percentage of patients, often women, are diagnosed with fibromyalgia.

Fibromyalgia is a disorder causing chronic muscle pain, tenderness, and fatigue. This disorder was not well defined until 1992. Prior to that time, these symptoms were often classified under a catch-all diagnosis of "chronic pain syndrome."

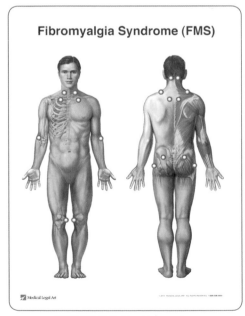

Fibromyalgia Syndrome (FMS)

Medical Legal Art

©1997-2010 Medical Legal Art. www.doereport.com

A diagnosis of fibromyalgia is reached based upon a history of both widespread pain and pain response to finger pressure in 11 to 18 specific tender point sites. Widespread pain occurs when all of the following are present:

❊ pain in both sides of the body;

❊ pain above and below the waist;

❊ pain in the axial skeletal (bones of the head, spine and torso).

The cause of fibromyalgia has not been conclusively established within the scientific community. However, contemporary studies do provide support for the following assertions.

RICHARD H. ADLER
Attorney at Law, Adler Giersch PS

1. **Psychological factors.** There is no basis for the statement that the pain and tenderness in fibromyalgia patients are primarily caused by emotional stress, depression, or anxiety. However, there is agreement that these factors may, on occasion, increase or exacerbate the intensity of pain.

2. **Sleep disturbance.** Fibromyalgia patients often wake up without feeling refreshed or restored. Testing has revealed that this sleep disturbance is connected with an abnormal reading on a brain-wave study called an electroencephalogram, or EEG. There appears to be a disturbance of the deeper stages of sleep.

3. **Muscle tissues.** Biopsy of muscle tissues in fibromyalgia patients has failed to reveal any changes that are characteristic or diagnostic of the condition.

4. **Pain.** Recent evidence shows that fibromyalgia patients have an enhanced perception of pain that appears to be physically based.

5. **Increased sympathetic activity.** Fibromyalgia patients appear to have an increased sensitivity to normal stimulation. Most fibromyalgia patients complain of sensitivity to cold. Other complaints include dry eyes, dry mouth, fluid retention, and bladder irritability.

Though all specific causes of fibromyalgia have not been determined, studies have shown a link between traumatic injury and fibromyalgia. However, insurers consistently challenge traumatic injury as a cause of fibromyalgia.

Despite insurers' challenges, many doctors recognize trauma as a cause of the disorder. Fibromyalgia is a life-altering condition that affects all aspects of the patient's life. Common complaints and effects include:

1. **Localized muscle pain.**

2. **Functional disability**. Fibromyalgia patients will have problems with activities of daily living comparable to rheumatoid arthritis patients that include mobility, arm function, grip strength, and household tasks.

3. **Poor physical fitness.** When you hurt all over, all of the time, you are likely not inclined or able to exercise.

4. **Work disability.**

5. **Psychological distress.** When fibromyalgia is full blown, many individuals will present with depression, anxiety, and phobia. The psychological distress, however, is more a consequence of pain rather than a cause of it. Psychological distress compounds the situation but is not the primary cause of these symptoms.

6. **Decreased quality of life.** All parts of the person's life are affected, including health, relationships, and the ability to engage in recreational activities.

Treatment programs must be individualized and draw from a multidisciplinary approach, and they must focus on pain reduction, postural instruction, adjustments to restore spinal biomechanics, stretching and exercise, stress reduction, life-style changes to improve sleep, and appropriate medications. The most successful programs emphasize the patient's active participation. It is also critical that the patient's doctor be able to diagnose fibromyalgia correctly and early, as well as understand its consequences. Patient education is important so that patients know they have a chronic disorder that will require long-term treatment.

1. **Exercise and physical therapy.** There is a limited number of studies in this area. The best that can be said is that a low-impact, low-load exercise training program, such as brisk walking, biking, or swimming, with some psychological intervention, is recommended. The idea is to avoid the effects of inactivity on muscles, to increase endorphin secretion, and to provide the patient with some control over his or her activity level.

2. **Education.** One way to decrease patient anxiety and lead to better treatment compliance is for fibromyalgia patients to have a clear diagnosis and understanding of their condition. Many fibromyalgia patients may be dealing with their pain problems but have a physician who does not believe or understand the diagnosis at all. Getting a referral to a rheumatol-

ogist who understands fibromyalgia, its relationship to trauma, and potential treatment can go a long way in helping someone adjust to this medical condition.

3. **Medications.** A variety of medications have been tried for the treatment of fibromyalgia. Many studies doubt the usefulness of medication because of the overall poor performance and significant side effects. There is little evidence that medication results in prolonged pain relief. However, there are some clinical therapeutic trials demonstrating that low dosages of tricylic medications are more effective than placebos in the treatment of fibromyalgia. The largest controlled studies have been with Amitriptyline and Cyclobenzaprine.

4. **Homeopathy.** Tincture of poison oak diluted in ethanol has been the most commonly indicated homeopathic medicine for 42 percent of fibromyalgia patients. In one double-blind placebo trial, the patients receiving the tincture did better in all variables compared to patients taking placebos. The number of tender spots reduced by about a quarter. A significant improvement in pain and sleep was reported.

5. **Manipulation.** Though manipulation, such as chiropractic or osteopathic adjustments, does not appear to cure the condition, fibromyalgia patients frequently report temporary pain relief following manipulation, but a return of symptoms thereafter. One author has theorized that relief may be due to a reduction of muscle tension, a release of endorphins, a reduction of stress, a correction of postural dysfunction, or other unknown mechanisms. More research is underway in this area.

Court Decisions

When a claim is being made by the attorney for the injured person that the trauma caused fibromyalgia, or aggravated an existing condition, the attorney must produce evidence which supports a positive answer to two key questions:

1. Whether the condition is real; and

2. Whether the condition arose from the traumatic injury in the case.

The answer to the first question is clear, and evidenced by noting that a majority of the medical community, insurers, and the federal government agree that fibromyalgia is a real, debilitating condition. The response to the second question on causation can be more difficult to prove, as there is no consensus on the relationship of trauma to the development of fibromyalgia.

There are significant studies showing a link between trauma and fibromyalgia, both in the context of a single traumatic injury event, as well as in the context of repetitive injuries. However, at the heart of the causation issue is this simple statement, in materials posted on the National Institute of Arthritis and Musculoskeletal and Skin Diseases website, summing up the current understanding of fibromyalgia and its relationship to trauma

> The causes of fibromyalgia are unknown. There may be a number of factors involved.

Disappointing, to say the least. But in order for a condition to be allowed into evidence and considered as part of a traumatic personal injury claim, it must be shown more probably true than not that the condition arose because of, was aggravated by, or made symptomatic due to the injury incident at issue in the case.

In order to establish in court that a traumatic incident caused fibromyalgia, your attorney must satisfy certain rules designed to insure that the evidence submitted is reliable and generally accepted in the medical community.

The insurance company and their attorney will challenge the admissibility of such evidence by claiming there is a lack of established and generally accepted support in the medical community at large for the assertion that traumatic injury causes individuals to develop fibromyalgia.

While state and federal courts have not been uniform in deciding the causal question, many courts have not allowed injured plaintiffs to assert that their condition, treatment costs, and other damages were caused by traumatic fibromyalgia. State courts in Nebraska, Minnesota, Indiana, and Florida have ruled evidence of trauma causing fibromyalgia may not be entered into evidence, as have two federal circuit courts. However, they have also left the door open as one court quoted fibromyalgia researcher Dr. Thomas J. Romano, who stated:

> Clearly when entities such as the American Academy of Pain Management as well as numerous other doctors have formally stated that trauma may cause fibromyalgia, the concept that trauma may cause fibromyalgia is a solid one. *Marsh v. Valyou.*[1]

Further, as another court noted:

> In reaching this decision, this court does not hold that trauma does not cause fibromyalgia or that admission of such evidence is forever barred, only that at the current time the medical science linking such a causal relationship does not exist.

Washington State courts apply the standard from *Frye v. United States*,[2] to decide whether or not expert testimony on novel scientific theories may be admitted in court. To be admissible, the offering party must show the underlying theory is generally accepted in the scientific community and that there are techniques, experiments, or studies utilizing that theory which are capable of producing reliable results.

In *Grant v. Boccia*,[3] a 2006 Washington appeals court first held that relating fibromyalgia to trauma was a novel scientific theory to which the *Frye* rule applied. It then went on to hold that, because the causal relationship between trauma and fibromyalgia has *not* been decisively established in the medical literature, it is not generally accepted in the relevant scientific community. Accordingly, expert testimony linking the injured person's fibromyalgia to an automobile collision was excluded as evidence by the trial judge.

Another Court of Appeals decision, after *Grant v. Boccia*, involved an Okanogan County trial judge admitting into evidence expert medical testimony both for and against traumatically induced fibromyalgia from a motor vehicle injury case. Interestingly, when later deciding on multiple issues on appeal in that case, the appeals court recited the fact that testimony regarding fibromyalgia was admitted as evidence

---

1   917 So.2d 313 (Fla.App. 5 Dist. 2005)

2   293 F. 1013, 54 App. D.C. 46 (D.C.Cir.1923)

3   133 Wn.App. 176, 137 P.3d 20 (2006)

by the trial court, without comment as to whether or not it should have been admitted and considered by the jury in reaching their verdict (*Herriman v. May*[4]).

Fortunately, a more recent decision from the Washington Supreme Court in the case of *Anderson v. Alzo Nobel Coatings, Inc.*,[5] in the latter part of 2011, overruled the Court of Appeals' decision in *Grant v. Boccia* regarding the *Frye*-standard and the admissibility of medical scientific evidence. The *Grant* decision required that there must be a 'consensus of opinion' within the relevant medical community on the theory of causation to be admitted into evidence. But the Supreme Court in *Anderson* ruled that a consensus of opinion on the causation theory was not required. Rather the theory of the connection between the trauma and the injury 'must be based on principals and methods which are generally accepted within the community'.

Under *Anderson*, there is room in Washington's law for the recognition of fibromyalgia as a traumatically induced and/or aggravated pre-existing condition for which patients should be fairly compensated. Fibromyalgia is a recognized condition for which treatment will be paid by insurance.

When presenting a traumatically induced fibromyalgia claim, it is critical that all types of diagnoses get explored, and all applicable conditions be documented.

If you are involved in a motor vehicle collision, a trip and fall incident, or pedestrian, bicycle, or construction site injury, and you have chronic pain symptoms, have your family physician refer you to a specialist in rheumatology or one otherwise familiar with fibromyalgia.

---

4 142 Wash.App. 226, 174 P.3d 156 (2007)
5 260 P.3rd 857 (2011)

RICHARD H. ADLER
Attorney at Law, Adler Giersch PS

REFLEX SYMPATHETIC DYSTROPHY SYNDROME (RSDS)

CHAPTER 47

Reflex Sympathetic Dystrophy Syndrome (RSDS) is a chronic pain disorder involving the *sympathetic nervous system*. Just how the sympathetic nervous system controls the underlying cause of RSDS has not been defined, but abnormalities of the sympathetic nervous system have been strongly implicated.

Usually RSDS develops after a traumatic injury. RSDS can also be a complication of surgery, infection, casting, splinting, or myocardial infarction (heart attack). The condition has been defined as synonymous with Complex Regional Pain Syndrome, Type I (CRPS). There are several considerations in understanding RSDS:

Early recognition of the syndrome and prompt treatment, ideally within three months of the first symptoms, provides the greatest opportunity for effective recovery.

1. RSDS/CRPS is a chronic pain syndrome most often resulting from trauma to an arm or leg;

2. RSDS/CRPS patients report burning, aching, searing pain that is initially localized at the site of the injury. The involved area usually has increased sensitivity to touch. The pain syndrome may appear to be out of proportion to the inciting traumatic injury;

3. Inappropriate or exaggerated neural signals are sent to the brain that may then misinterpret nonpainful stimuli as painful;

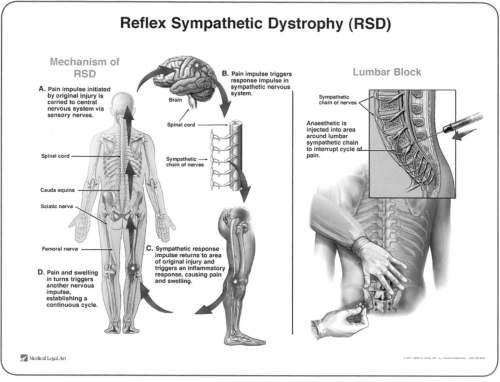

Reflex Sympathetic Dystrophy (RSD)

Mechanism of RSD

A. Pain impulse initiated by original injury is carried to central nervous system via sensory nerves.

B. Pain impulse triggers response impulse in sympathetic nervous system.

Lumbar Block

Brain

Spinal cord

Spinal cord

Sympathetic chain of nerves

Cauda equina

Sciatic nerve

Femoral nerve

C. Sympathetic response impulse returns to area of original injury and triggers an inflammatory response, causing pain and swelling.

D. Pain and swelling in turns triggers another nervous impulse, establishing a continuous cycle.

Sympathetic chain of nerves

Anaesthetic is injected into area around lumbar sympathetic chain to interrupt cycle of pain.

Medical Legal Art

©1997-2010 Medical Legal Art. www.doereport.com

4. Early recognition of the syndrome and prompt treatment, ideally within three months of the first symptoms, provides the greatest opportunity for effective recovery;

5. RSDS/CRPS often affects an individual's ability to perform sustained work activity; and

6. Signs and symptoms of RSDS/CRPS can persist longer than twelve months and, in many cases, lasts for years.

It is important to add that many of these symptoms are not static. They undergo dynamic changes over time, and several examinations may be required before the condition can be properly documented. Also, RSDS/CRPS, when documented by accepted medical standards and lasting for twelve months or longer, can be the basis for a finding of disability.

If you or someone you know has the signs and symptoms of RSDS or has been diagnosed with it, an immediate referral to a specialist is recommended to confirm the diagnosis and begin intervention.

While RSDS/CRPS symptoms result from traumatic injury or from surgery (if necessitated by traumatic injury), they may present you with a host of insurance and legal challenges.

While RSDS/CRPS symptoms result from traumatic injury or from surgery (if necessitated by traumatic injury), they may present you with a host of insurance and legal challenges.

IMAGING TESTS

CHAPTER 48

When you have traumatic injuries, it is critical to get them evaluated immediately so that the source of pain and limitations can be determined. Pain and limitations of movement can be caused by many different types of injuries and there is often an overlap of symptoms coming from different pain sources.

For example, is the neck pain and numbness that spreads down into your shoulder and into your arm coming from the nerves, disc, facet, ligament, muscle, or tendon tissue? Determining the source of the injury helps direct the next steps in treatment. The adage applies: Before you can have a cure, you need the correct diagnosis.

Before you can have a cure, you need the correct diagnosis.

When healthcare providers look to diagnose traumatic injuries, they rely upon diagnostic imaging to see inside the body.

When healthcare providers look to diagnose traumatic injuries, they rely upon diagnostic imaging to see inside the body. The most common imaging tools include X-rays, CT scans, MRIs, and bone scans.

A. X-Rays

Plain X-ray films are best at revealing bone and joint spacing abnormalities. They are used most often to assess or rule out a broken bone or joint dislocation. X-rays are also useful in showing the alignment of the bony structures of a joint or the space within the joint to determine whether there is arthritis or degeneration in the area. X-rays can be useful to a chiropractor assessing the alignment of the spinal column or a region of the spine.

X-rays are the most familiar form of diagnostic imaging. When X-ray radiation is transmitted through the body, various areas of the film or digital plate placed behind the object will lighten or darken, depending upon the tissue density through which the beam has passed. Solid bone, which is denser than tissues, absorbs X-ray radiation so that the film is less exposed and appears lighter. Muscles, tissues, ligaments, and various body organs

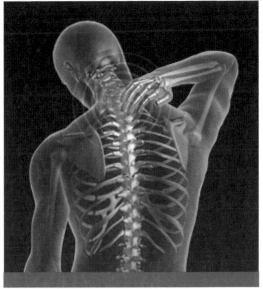

©iStockphoto.com/Mads Abildgaard

are predominately the same density and thus are not readily distinguished from one another. As a result they yield little or no detail on X-ray film; therefore X-rays are not very useful in assessing soft-tissue trauma.

When an X-ray film is interpreted as negative (normal) it only means that there is no broken bone or joint dislocation. But a negative X-ray does not rule out injuries to soft tissues such as a disc, facet, cartilage, muscle, ligament, etc.

Therefore, an X-ray finding that is negative because it cannot show soft-tissue injury does not mean there is no injury, despite the contrary argument by insurance claim representatives. A negative X-ray finding when a patient has pain may lead the healthcare provider to continue to refine the diagnosis and order additional imaging tests.

Other significant X-rays findings include the integrity and alignment of the spinal column, the flattening of the cervical spine, or the straightening of the normal curve of the neck in lateral (side view) projection on X-ray. Muscles frequently respond to injury by spasming. Since the muscles are attached to the individual vertebrae, muscle spasms may be reflected by the change in the configuration of the spine, a reversal of the normal curve or straightening of the spine due to the pulling of the muscle. Changes in the spine structure clearly document the presence of muscle spasms secondary to an injury.

The presence of arthritis or degenerative changes to the bone, seen in various X-ray films, include osteophytes, narrow interverebral disc spaces, and calcified ligaments. Such abnormal structures are more prone to damage than normal tissue and lack normal recovery abilities. As a result, injuries to these already abnormal areas can produce more significant acute symptoms, take longer to heal, and will generally result in an ongoing disability.

Although plain film digital X-rays demonstrate some clinically relevant information, there are inherent limitations with demonstrating conditions such as disc herniations, spinal stenosis, and subtle or non-displaced fractures.

B. CT Scan

Computed Tomography (CT or "CAT" Scan) is a rapid diagnostic examination that combines X-rays and computers.

The images produced by CT scans are computer-generated rather than formed directly by electromagnetic radiation, as in X-rays. A computer digitally constructs an image based upon the measurements of the absorption of the X-rays through the body part being examined. CT scans can provide pictures that look like slices through a body – such as when you slice raisin bread and can see where the raisins are. During CT imaging, the X-ray source rotates around your body, and each rotation produces a single cross-sectional "slice," like slices in a loaf of bread. CT scans allow physicians to see a horizontal picture of the body. A CT scan allows the radiologist to see the location, nature, and extent of many different diseases or abnormalities inside the body. CT scans can be used to obtain information about almost any organ, blood vessels, abdominal cavity, bones, and the spinal cord. CT scans are

A lesion in the body generally has to be 1.0 to 1.5 centimeter to be visualized by CT scan. There can be brain bleeding or nerve irritation with no visible change on a CT scan if the bleed occurs at the microscopic level.

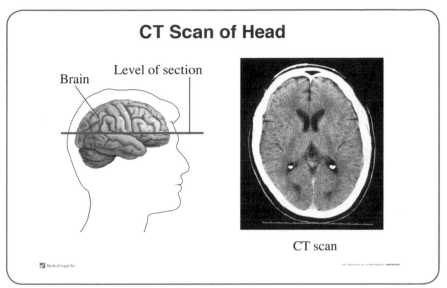

CT Scan of Head

Brain

Level of section

CT scan

Medical Legal Art

©1997-2010 Medical Legal Art. www.doereport.com

often the preferred imaging tests in the emergency room because they can be administered quickly and identify bleeding or clotting at traumatic injury sites.

CT scanning, however, has limitations. CT scans show only structural damage and accumulation of fluid, and have a lower resolution than an MRI. A lesion in the body generally has to be 1.0 to 1.5 centimeter to be visualized by CT scan. There can be brain bleeding or nerve irritation with no visible change on a CT scan if the bleed occurs at the microscopic level.

C. MRI

MRI stands for Magnetic Resonance Imaging, a technique used to show abnormalities of soft tissues in finer detail and greater clarity than CT scans. Large magnetic or radio waves are used instead of X-rays to take pictures of the body's tissues. With today's MRI, a patient is placed on their back and slid into the MRI scanning device. The device uses super cooled electric coils made of titanium alloys to generate a powerful, vertical magnetic field, which is held at a constant strength measured in Tesla units. The body part imaged responds to the magnetic field because the body is composed of 90 percent water that is made up of

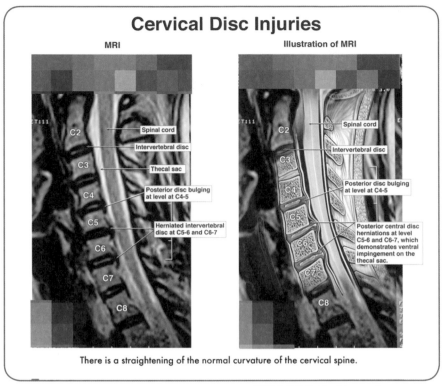

Cervical Disc Injuries

| MRI | Illustration of MRI |

MRI labels: C2, C3, C4, C5, C6, C7, C8; Spinal cord; Intervertebral disc; Thecal sac; Posterior disc bulging at level at C4-5; Herniated intervertebral disc at C5-6 and C6-7

Illustration of MRI labels: C2, C3, C4, C5, C6, C7, C8; Spinal cord; Intervertebral disc; Posterior disc bulging at level at C4-5; Posterior central disc herniations at level C5-6 and C6-7, which demonstrates ventral impingement on the thecal sac.

There is a straightening of the normal curvature of the cervical spine.

©1997-2010 Medical Legal Art. www.doereport.com

molecules of hydrogen and oxygen, which carry a single proton in each atom of hydrogen. Protons are constantly spinning in their natural state, but the magnet temporarily stops the spinning. A radio frequency signal is bounced off the protons just as the magnet releases them. The changes from the spinning water protons in your body are recorded, digitized, and used by the computer to reconstruct a 3-dimensional image showing the location and appearance of soft tissue and fluids. MRIs are used because they provide detailed pictures of organs, discs, and soft tissues to diagnose a variety of medical conditions. MRIs are commonly requested by doctors to diagnose key areas of the body such as head/brain, spine, bone/joints, chest, and abdomen.

Because of the intense magnetic fields used in the MRI scanner, the technician will have you remove all metal, jewelry, watches, hair clips, etc. prior to the scan. It is important to let the MRI technician know about any prior surgeries or metal implants such as a pacemaker, joint replacements, etc.

Every MRI scanner has what is called "field strength" or the power of the scanner's magnet. Higher field strength means that your MRI scan will be clearer and show smaller details of your body. Typically, MRI field strengths are at 1.5 T, 2.0 T, and 3.0 T. The 3.0 T scanners are the newest and therefore not as widely available. However, because evidence of traumatic injuries is critical to establish your claim, it is wisest to get the strongest MRI scan available. The clearer the image, the easier it is for your doctor to make an accurate and decisive diagnoses of your traumatic injuries, and that is critical to recommending the proper treatment options available to you. And all of this provides clearer evidence of your injuries for claim evaluation purposes.

Open MRI scanners are available for those with severe claustrophobia or for larger-framed individuals. However, most healthcare professional prefer the closed scanners as they provide a higher field strength and therefore better clarity. The MRI is best suited to revealing soft tissue disease, spinal cord injury, disc herniation, ligament injury, etc. The anatomy of the brain is well demonstrated with an MRI. MRI scanners cannot reveal pictures at the cellular level of the brain or show diffuse cellular brain damage (see page 165–167 for information on diffuse axonal injury) from a shear-strain injury. MRI machines can only visualize brain tissue of 1.5 mm. At this level, there remain billions of brain cells that cannot be seen.

As a result, a great majority of patients diagnosed with mild traumatic brain injury have negative (normal) MRIs. It's important to remember that a negative MRI does not by itself rule out traumatic brain injury.

D. fMRI

Functional MRI, or fMRI, is a type of specialized MRI scan. It measures the tiny metabolic changes in the blood that take place in the brain when a specific task is performed. It is one of the most recently developed forms of neuroimaging, allowing the ability to observe both the structure of the brain and which structures participate and relate to specific tasks. This new ability to observe allows the specialist to determine

An fMRI measures the tiny metabolic changes in the blood that take place in the brain when a specific task is performed.

which part of the brain is handling functions such as thought, speech, movement, and sensation. This is becoming an increasingly important tool in assessing the effects of trauma on brain function.

E. Bone Scan

The bones inside your body are alive and active, providing support for your body and serving as your body's warehouse for important minerals. Inside the long bones is a soft core called bone marrow that manufactures blood cells.

The process of bone growth and renewal is part of your body's metabolism, a natural process that creates and uses energy. Changes in your bone metabolism can be caused by a number of problems. To get a picture of your bone metabolism, your doctor may order a test called a bone scan. The radiologist or medical specialist will be able to see any abnormalities in metabolism on images from a bone scan. Your doctor may also order a bone scan to help diagnose subtle or hidden bone fractures such as a stress fracture that may not show up on a routine X-ray. Also, your doctor my order a bone scan to determine whether you have any bone abnormalities that may signify problems such as arthritis, infection of the joint, avascular necrosis (impaired bone blood supply), or any unexplained pain that may originate from the bone. Bone scans are also ordered to help rule out other causes of pain, such as tumor or cancer.

F. SPECT Scan

A Single Photon Emission Computed Tomography (SPECT) scan is a type of nuclear imaging test that shows how blood flows to tissues or organs.

The test is started by injecting a chemical dye that can be seen by the scanner. The computer collects the information and converts it into 2-dimensional cross sections. These cross sections are then added together to form a 3-D image of the brain or spine.

A SPECT scan is primarily used to view how blood flows through arteries and veins in the brain and organs such as your heart. With a SPECT Scan the rate of blood flow to your heart or body's organ tells us whether it is more or less active.

TREATMENT OPTIONS

In general, medical treatments are designed to improve function of an injured area by focusing on strength, range of motion, flexibility, endurance, and pain reduction. There are many treatment options available such as chiropractic adjustments, physical therapy, acupuncture, massage therapy, epidural steroid injections, facet injections, trigger point injections, radio frequency rhizotomy, and surgery, to name just a few. Every patient's treatment regimen will be unique to their situation and needs.

Not all therapies are appropriate for all injuries. Primary care physicians (PCPs) referring you for treatment may have favorite forms of therapy and may frown on other types. Different PCPs will approach the same problem from their unique perspective. However, it's important to understand your treatment options, particularly when one form of care is not reducing pain or increasing your function. It is important to examine other treatment options that may be available. For example, if you are treating a neck injury and were diagnosed on MRI with a disc bulge that also caused radiating pain in your arm, but it did not improve with time, rest, or medication, it would be appropriate to ask your doctor for additional therapies, or to refer you to another doctor for a second opinion. By having more than

> *There are many treatment options available. Every patient's treatment regimen will be unique to their situation and needs.*

one type of treatment option available, you are more likely to have success increasing your function and decreasing pain. The trick is to recognize when adequate progress is not being made with one type of therapy.

A. Chiropractic Care

Chiropractors are licensed healthcare professionals specializing mainly in spinal manipulation to restore alignment of the vertebrae

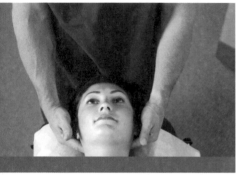

©iStockphoto.com/Rich Legg

in the spine and improve normal nervous-system functions. Chiropractors hold a four-year degree as a Doctor of Chiropractic, with the designation "D.C." following their name. Following chiropractic college, there are options to continue on with post–graduate training in "diplomate" programs in sports, nutrition, orthopedics, radiology, and neurology. Multiple published studies regarding patient satisfaction with chiropractic care has led to its use in a more mainstream manner.

Advances made in chiropractic techniques have changed the opinions of many who now believe that chiropractic care may be the preferred choice for the management of musculoskeletal problems.

Chiropractic is a healthcare approach that focuses on the relationship between the body structure – mainly the spine – and its functioning. Although practitioners may use a variety of treatment techniques, the primary focus for the chiropractor is to perform adjustments to the spine or other joints of the body with the goal of correcting alignment problems and supporting the body's natural ability to heal itself. People generally seek chiropractic care for conditions such as neck pain, back pain, and headaches. The chiropractic adjustment involves using the hands or a device to apply a controlled force to a joint, moving it beyond its passive range of motion. The goal is to increase the range and quality of motion in the area being treated and to aid in restoring health. Chiropractors combine the use of spinal adjustments with several other treatment approaches such as mobilization, heat and ice, rest, rehabilitative exercises, counseling about diet, weight loss, lifestyle, and dietary supplements.

There is increasing data supporting the effectiveness of chiropractic care and patient satisfaction.

A 2009 Consumer Reports reader survey found "hands on" therapies, led by chiropractic care, were the top-rated treatment for back pain suffers, with chiropractic receiving the highest satisfaction-with-care ratings.

A study in the June 2010 issue of the *Journal of the American Board of Family Medicine*[1], based on data from the 2002 National Health Interview Survey, revealed that 60 percent of U.S. adults utilizing hands-on therapies for back pain reported "a great deal" of benefit. Chiropractic was used most frequently, at 74 percent, and had the highest success rate.

B. Physical Therapy

Physical therapy is a healthcare speciality concerned with treating disorders of the musculoskeletal system and joints of the body such as the shoulder, hip, knee, ankle, and wrist, and their interaction with physical movement. Physical therapists are licensed professionals who hold a master's degree and sometimes a doctor's degree in physical therapy. They work in a variety of settings including hospitals, rehabilitation clinics, outpatient facilities, and nursing homes.

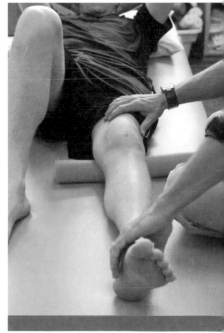

©iStockphoto.com/Tammy Bryngelson

The ultimate goal of physical therapy is to restore maximum functional independence to each individual patient. To achieve this, treatment may include exercise,

---

1   Kanodia AK, Legedza ATR, Davis RB, et al. Perceived benefit of complementary and alternative medicine (CAM) for back pain: a national survey. J AM Board of Fam Med 2010, 23: 354-62

> *The **ultimate goal** of physical therapy is to restore maximum functional independence to each individual patient.*

heat, cold, electrical stimulation, and massage. Physical therapists as well as chiropractors will use neuromuscular re-education, and include therapies that improve reflexes, balance, coordination, posture, and activities that promote better movement.

C. Massage Therapy

Massage therapy from a licensed massage practitioner is one of the oldest healing arts performed. Today the benefits of massage are varied and far reaching. As an accepted part of any physical rehabilitation program, massage therapy has proven beneficial for many chronic pain conditions including low back pain, neck pain, as well as injuries to various joints of the body. As those who have received one know, massage helps relieve the stress and tension of everyday living that can lead to health complications.

There are dozens of variations of massage, body work, and therapies practiced by massage practitioners. They included stroking, kneading, tapping, deep tissue compression, vibration, lymph drainage, rocking, friction, and pressure to the muscular structures of soft tissues in the human body. This may also include

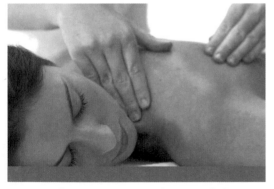

non-forceful passive or active motion and their application of techniques intended to affect the energetic systems of the body. The benefits of massage include reducing stress, encouraging relaxation, improving posture, relaxing muscle tissues, improving flexibility and range of motion, breaking up scar tissue from prolonged immobilization, reducing headaches, enhancing post-surgical rehabilitation, improving rehabilitation following trauma, and managing pain or chronic conditions. A massage therapist is not allowed to evaluate and diagnose healthcare conditions, but your medical doctor or chiropractor can.

All licensed massage therapy is covered under all automobile Personal Injury Protection (PIP) policies. Massage therapy is also covered under most health insurance plans, but there may be a limit on the number of sessions permitted in a calendar year, or your therapist may not be accepted as a provider in your health insurance plan.

As those who have received one know, massage helps relieve the stress and tension of everyday living that can lead to health complications.

However, many experienced massage therapists offering injury-related massage will often work with their patient on a lien (promise to pay at the conclusion of the case when there is a settlement) when a patient's PIP or health insurance benefits are exhausted or no longer available.

D. Acupuncture

Acupuncture is widely practiced in the United States and throughout the world as a therapeutic intervention for numerous disease processes including traumatic and non-traumatic musculoskeletal injuries and neurological deficits. Acupuncture has proven to be effective for relief and resolution of acute and chronic pain related to musculoskeletal injuries.

Acupuncture is becoming more widely practiced in traditional medical and naturopathic communities to treat chronic pain syndromes or other injuries.

Physicians who devote themselves to providing relief to chronic pain patients with traumatic injuries have increasingly turned to acupuncture as a safe, effective, and relatively non-invasive therapy.

Acupuncture involves the insertion of very fine needles, sometime along with electrical stimulation or heat, on the body's surface in order to influence internal functions. Findings from basic research shed light on the mechanisms of acupuncture and include the release of chemicals within the central nervous system to improve immune response, circulation, and controlling the pathways of pain. Acupuncture can be effective in an overall comprehensive program of physical rehabili-

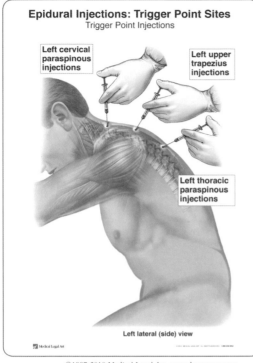

Epidural Injections: Trigger Point Sites
Trigger Point Injections

Left cervical paraspinous injections

Left upper trapezius injections

Left thoracic paraspinous injections

Left lateral (side) view

Medical Legal Art

©1997-2010 Medical Legal Art. www.doereport.com

tation and chiropractic care to return a traumatically injured person to their activities of daily living, particularly when other treatment approaches have not resulted in sufficient pain reduction or improved function.

E. Trigger Point Injections

When various conservative, non-invasive therapies such as chiropractic care, physical therapy, massage therapy, or acupuncture do not sufficiently reduce pain and increase function, healthcare providers may turn to semi-invasive procedures involving injections.

Trigger points are tight knots of muscles that form when muscles fail to relax. Trigger point injections are performed by injecting a local anesthetic (numbing medication) with or without an anti-inflammatory medication, such as a steroid, to relax the muscle, thereby reducing pain.

When pain is reduced, motion is increased and may lead to retrials of therapies that were not previously successful. Such injections are often directed toward specific areas of the spine to treat headaches, muscle spasms, limited range of motion, etc.

F. Facet Joint Injection

A facet joint injection is given when the doctor believes the source of irritation is in the small joints in a painful segment of the spine.

These injections are often tried after manual approaches of chiropractic, physical therapy, massage, or acupuncture have not sufficiently reduced your pain and increased your function. The facet joints provide stability and help guide spinal motion. A facet injection to the neck, middle back, or low back involves injecting a steroid (anti-inflammatory medication) that numbs the facet joint and blocks the pain.

A facet injection to the neck, middle back, or low back involves injecting a steroid (anti-inflammatory medication) that numbs the facet joint and blocks the pain.

If multiple levels of pain exist within the facets, several injections over time may be required to pinpoint the pain source. Once your pain has been relieved, your doctor may recommend a retrial of those manual therapies that did not initially cure the condition. With less pain, you will have less restriction and limitations of motion. The chiropractor, physical therapist, massage therapist, and/or acupuncturist can then work the area at a deeper level to increase motion, increase function,

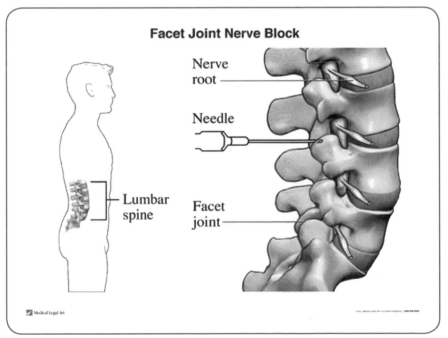

Facet Joint Nerve Block

Nerve root

Needle

Lumbar spine

Facet joint

Medical Legal Art

©1997-2010 Medical Legal Art. www.doereport.com

decrease pain, and stabilize the area.

G. Epidural Steroid Injection

Epidural steroid injections both treat and help diagnose the condition of a pinched nerve or torn disc. Local anesthetic (numbing medication) and an anti-inflammatory steroid medication are delivered into the spinal area on the surface of the spinal column (where a nerve or disc is believed to be irritated). This type of injection may reduce

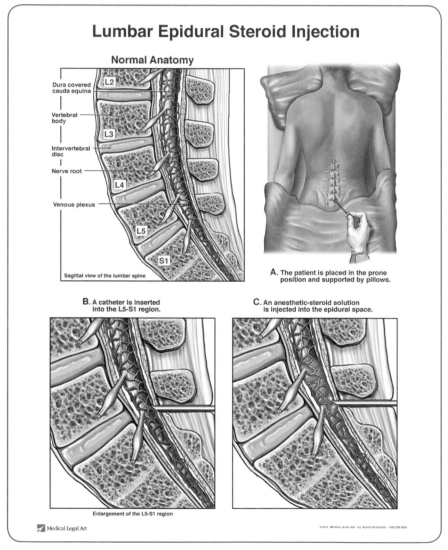

Lumbar Epidural Steroid Injection

Normal Anatomy

Dura covered cauda equina

Vertebral body

Intervertebral disc

Nerve root

Venous plexus

L2

L3

L4

L5

S1

Sagittal view of the lumbar spine

A. The patient is placed in the prone position and supported by pillows.

B. A catheter is inserted into the L5-S1 region.

C. An anesthetic-steroid solution is injected into the epidural space.

Enlargement of the L5-S1 region

Medical Legal Art

©1997-2010 Medical Legal Art. www.doereport.com

inflammation, resulting in long-term pain relief, and can also provide valuable information about the source of pain. Using a very thin needle and a moving digital X-ray for guidance, the medical specialist will inject a dye into or next to the spinal space thought to be causing your pain. This ensures the correct placement of the needle for the procedure. X-rays are taken and a combination of anti-inflammatory and anesthetic medications are then injected for pain relief. Patients often report a sensation of numbness and/ or pain relief for up to six hours immediately after the injection. Symptoms usually return after the short-term anesthetic wears off and before the long-term steroid anti-inflammatory medication kicks in, typically about two

This type of injection may reduce inflammation, resulting in long-term pain relief, and can also provide valuable information about the source of pain.

to seven days later. If an initial epidural steroid injection produces relief, a second injection might be recommended to strengthen the long-term relief. If the pain returns, another injection can be recommended, but a specialist in this area will not generally recommend more than three epidural steroid injections in one year.

If there is no change to your symptoms after a few weeks following the injection, your doctor may want to investigate other potential causes of pain and look at a second injection that may be different than the initial one.

H. Radio Frequency Rhizotomy or Neurotomy

A radio frequency (RF) rhizotomy, also known as a neurotomy, is an advanced spinal intervention designed to decrease and/or eliminate pain symptoms arising from the facet joints within the spine, when all other non-invasive measures have failed. The procedure involves destroying the nerve that enters (innervates) the facet joints with highly localized heat generated by radio waves delivered by a very thin needle. By destroying the nerve, the communication link that signals pain from the spine to the brain can be disrupted.

Before a radio frequency rhizotomy can be scheduled, it is important for your doctor to clearly identify the specific areas where the pain originates. Testing and treatment required to determine the specific

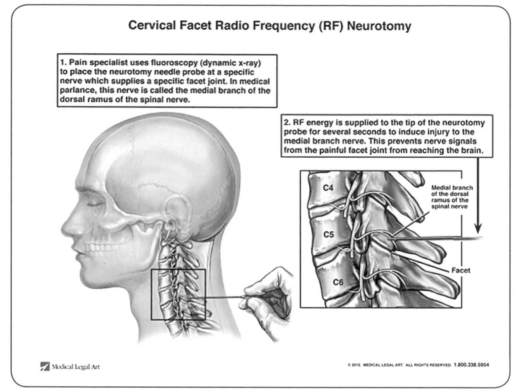

Cervical Facet Radio Frequency (RF) Neurotomy

1. Pain specialist uses fluoroscopy (dynamic x-ray) to place the neurotomy needle probe at a specific nerve which supplies a specific facet joint. In medical parlance, this nerve is called the medial branch of the dorsal ramus of the spinal nerve.

2. RF energy is supplied to the tip of the neurotomy probe for several seconds to induce injury to the medial branch nerve. This prevents nerve signals from the painful facet joint from reaching the brain.

C4

C5

C6

Medial branch of the dorsal ramus of the spinal nerve

Facet

Medical Legal Art

nerve generating pain includes a comprehensive examination, an MRI of the spine, and a trial of facet injections.

During the rhizotomy, you must to be awake. The medical specialist will place a very thin needle electrode next to the facet joint generating the pain. The doctor will then check the needle placement with an X-ray camera, which is connected to a digital screen. To verify that the needle is in the correct position, the nerve may be stimulated using very low voltage electricity to cause the muscle to contract. Then the nerve receives numbing medication to put it to sleep. Finally, the doctor will apply heat to the nerve via the electrode for about one minute. The heat is designed to burn the nerve, which in turn breaks the communication link to the brain. The procedure is then repeated at the level above and below the facet previously determined as the pain generator. This is because of the inter-relationship of the nerve at the levels above and below the main source of the problem.

Improvement is usually noticed at the two to three week mark after the procedure; however, it could take up to four weeks before there is noticeable decrease in pain. One study has indicated that about 10 percent of patients can feel increased pain up to four weeks after the procedure, before the pain relief starts. Following a rhizotomy procedure, it is common for your doctor to recommend that you re-enter therapies such as chiropractic care, physical therapy, massage care, or acupuncture treatment so that additional

The procedure involves destroying the nerve that enters (innervates) the facet joints with highly localized heat generated by radio waves delivered by a very thin needle. By destroying the nerve, the communication link that signals pain from the spine to the brain can be disrupted.

gains can be made with increasing spinal motion, reducing scar tissue, and ensuring better joint mobility and stabilization.

I. Surgery

Surgery is only performed immediately after trauma if the injury is life-threatening or if not performing surgery could lead to worse outcomes such as loss of limb, deformity, or greater risk of worsening the condition. Otherwise, surgery is reserved for a later point in time following the trauma after all conservative measures have been exhausted and diagnostic tests and physical examinations point to surgery as the last, best alternative to reduce pain and increase function.

When surgery is recommended, it is a good idea to obtain a second opinion from another qualified surgeon. When selecting your surgeon, look for three traits: first, you want a surgeon who is regarded by other doctors as accomplished, experienced and reputable. Second, look for a surgeon with good bedside manner. Remember, in a traumatic injury case your doctors *may* need to testify at a deposition or trial. A good bedside manner will translate into the likeability and acceptability of their opinions. Finally, you want a surgeon who does not work directly for the insurance company. It may be hard to determine this without asking your attorney about your surgeon's background. Simply ask your surgeon whether he/she agrees with you that surgery is necessary because of your traumatic injury. Listen closely to his/her response, as it will tell you whether your doctor is clearly connecting the traumatic incident and your need for surgery. This is often an area that can lead to significant miscommunication and misunderstanding between the surgeon and patient.

CHILDREN AND TRAUMATIC INJURIES

CHAPTER 50

Recognizing the needs and vulnerabilities of children, both the law and medicine have special methods by which children are treated following a traumatic injury. Washington laws require special handling and rules related to children's claims.

Washington laws require special handling and rules related to children's claims.

In medicine, consideration of the difference between children and adults comes into play in diagnosis and treatment. Depending upon the age of the child, communication may be difficult. A child may describe a symptom with limited vocabulary. A symptom an adult would describe as "blurred vision," for instance, may be described by a child as "foamy" or some other descriptor. More importantly, a child may answer in the negative to a query about a specific symptom simply because they do not know what the word means, or may be too embarrassed to say yes. Specialized healthcare providers who understand the communication differences are important in getting accurate subjective information on which to base a diagnosis and then move forward with proper treatment.

©iStockphoto.com/Moodboard_Images

Physiological differences are also important to address in

RICHARD H. ADLER
Attorney at Law, Adler Giersch PS

treatment. An orthopedic injury such as a fracture, for example, must take into consideration the further growth of the bone in addressing the best form of treatment. Inappropriate repair of a fracture could lead to an adverse impact on the bone's growth and lead to long-term problems as the child grows. Pediatric specialists in virtually every practice area are generally accessible in populated areas and should be consulted when a child has suffered a traumatic injury.

Likewise, the legal system recognizes different standards of conduct for children and the unique vulnerabilities, incapacities, and limitations of this group. Washington law allows additional time for bringing actions against a negligent party on behalf of a child, and dictates who may bring and settle such a claim for a child.

A. Standards of Care and Statute of Limitations

In negligence actions, a child's conduct is not held to the same standard as an adult's. If a child causes an injury to another, he or she will be considered negligent only if the standard of the behavior falls below that of a reasonably careful child of the same age, intelligence, maturity, training, and experience.[1] Public policy recognizes that it would be unfair to hold a child's behavior to that of an adult. However, a 16- or 17-year-old may be held to an adult standard.

When a child is the harmed party, the three-year Statute of Limitations does not start until the child's 18th birthday. Then the child has three years from his or her 18th birthday to resolve the claim or file a lawsuit. The clock does not begin ticking right away as it does for an adult.

When a child is the one who has been harmed by the negligence of another, some special rules apply to pursuing damages. In Washington State, the period of time in which an action against a negligent party must be brought (named the Statute of Limitations law) is three years from the date of the occurrence. However, when a child is the harmed party, the three-year Statute of Limitations does not start until the child's 18th birthday. Then the child has three years from his or her 18th birthday

---

1   *Bauman by Chapman v. Crawford*, 104 Wash.2d 241, 704 P.2d 1181 (1985)

to resolve the claim or file a lawsuit. The clock does not begin ticking right away as it does for an adult.

B. Waivers

Despite the broad decision-making power of parents, there are instances in which the law does not allow a parent the final say. In

Though a parent may sign this type of waiver or release to allow their child to participate in an activity, Washington courts do not recognize them as valid.

Washington State, a person may sign away their right to bring an action for negligence against a potential party. The releases or waivers are a common occurrence when undertaking a recreational activity in which injury may occur. Though a parent may sign this type of waiver or release to allow their child to participate in an activity, Washington courts do not recognize them as valid.

In 1992, the Washington Supreme Court held these releases to be unenforceable because they violate public policy[2] and are contrary to the public good. In short, a parent may not sign away the legal rights of their children. However, the release may bar any claim by the parent for their own loss resulting from their child's injury.[3]

C. Minor's Personal Injury Settlement: Court Approval Required

When a case is concluded through settlement negotiations, Washington courts do not allow parents unfettered discretion.

When a claim is concluded for a minor Washington law requires that any tentative settlement be approved by a court, whether a lawsuit has been filed or not.

The court will appoint a specially trained representative called a *Guardian ad Litem* to review the facts of the case and provide a written opinion to the judge regarding the reasonableness of the proposed settlement. This protects the child from a parent potentially – perhaps

---

2   *Scott v. Pacific West Mountain Resort*, 119 Wash.2d 484, 834 P.2d 6 (1992)

3   Id.

through lack of knowledge – striking a bad deal. If approved, the court will generally require that the settlement funds of the child be placed in a blocked account. Money from the account cannot be withdrawn without a court order until the child turns 18.

When a child is the victim of a traumatic injury caused by another, it is important that he or she is treated by top healthcare specialists trained in evaluating and treating injuries to children. Only attorneys with experience and knowledge in understanding the special needs and requirements governing children and injury laws should be sought for representation.

PART FOUR

MOVING ON:
YOUR SETTLEMENT

SETTLEMENT — THE INSURANCE ADJUSTER IS NOT YOUR FRIEND

CHAPTER 51

The business model of an insurance company does not lend itself to compensating you based on what you think is reasonable or fair. The amount of compensation should be established with evidence. (But even when you have the evidence needed, it does not mean the responsible insurer will pay reasonable and fair compensation for your losses.)

The injured party has the burden to prove that the other party had a duty to act in a certain way, that there was a negligence of that duty, that the negligence caused an injury, and that the injury resulted in economic damages (medical expenses, loss of income, out of pocket expenses) and non-economic damages (inconvenience, pain and suffering, hassle-factors, loss of consortium).

The legal requirement that you prove your case is only one part of the settlement equation. The insurance company for the at-fault party also has a contractual and legal duty to protect its policy holder, their insured, from you, even when their negligence is crystal clear. A third part of the equation is that the insurer has its own business profit and shareholder concerns and this factor is often the overriding

Chris Ryan/OJO Images/Getty Images

consideration by an insurance company. These factors all mesh together to result in insurers paying the least amount on a claim that they can get away with, regardless of whether it seems fair and reasonable to you. At the same time, the liability insurer has a legal and contractual duty to protect the at-fault insured's interest so that there is no personal risk of a jury verdict greater than the insurance coverage available. This means that an insurance adjuster will attempt to settle your case for as little as possible, even if it means that the settlement offer is unreasonably low.

> *These factors all mesh together to result in insurers paying the least amount on a claim that they can get away with, regardless of whether it seems fair and reasonable to you.*

Insurance companies have developed several well-crafted strategies designed to minimize claim payouts. Some take advantage of the unequal bargaining power between the insurance company and an injured party without an attorney; others trick parties into a false sense of security. Some of these tactics have been exposed and ruled unlawful in courtrooms across the country.

One example of an overall deceptive business strategy comes from one of the largest insurance companies in the United States, Allstate. They adopted a confidential plan know as "Claims Core Process Redesign" (CCPR). This process is no longer confidential as it was the subject of many lawsuits, class actions, and investigations by Attorneys General and Insurance Commissioners around the country. The goal of this process was to enhance Allstate profits by having its claim representatives and adjusters target those individuals with traumatic injuries who had not retained an attorney. They then went to great lengths to encourage the unrepresented party to "trust" Allstate, and specifically and subtly influenced them not to seek any attorney's advice. Allstate trained its claim adjusters to establish an "empathetic trust based relationship" and "act as advocates" for unrepresented injured parties so they would not hire attorneys. Once the adjuster gained the unrepresented person's trust, the adjuster would recommend an intentionally undervalued settlement amount. Allstate's internal studies showed that by discouraging legal representation and cultivating trust it could persuade unrepresented people to settle for up to 50 percent less than what the company would pay if the injured party had legal representation.

The problem with Allstate's controversial plan was that it clearly established a conflict of interest as the company undertook to represent both its own insured (the at-fault party) as well as the injured party by advising each to trust Allstate and to not seek legal counsel. Allstate used its position and trained its adjusters to dupe and trick unrepresented traumatically injured people into accepting lowball settlement offers. Ultimately, Allstate's controversial policy generated a wave of litigation. State Attorneys General, State Bar Associations, and private individuals filed dozens of lawsuits against Allstate in 22 states alleging that these practices were fraudulent, deceptive, confusing, and illegal.

One case, *Jones v. Allstate Insurance Company*, started in Washington's King County Superior Court and made its way to the Washington Supreme Court, with a ruling in 2002. This case arose out of a claim for injuries filed by Janet Jones, who was seriously injured by an Allstate driver. Mrs. Jones' Chrysler minivan was broadsided by a 17-year-old Allstate driver, sending it rolling. Mrs. Jones suffered severe injuries to her head and face, and incurred bills totaling nearly $100,000.00. The Allstate adjuster, according to the company's business plan, contacted the Jones family and asked them to trust her – she promised to treat them as if they were her own clients. Allstate recommended that Mrs. Jones accept its offer of $25,000, as that was alleged to be the only insurance coverage available, leaving the Jones family with nearly $75,000 in additional medical bills. Jones signed the release. The release included Allstate, the at-fault driver, and the maker of Mrs. Jones's minivan. Interestingly, before the release was signed Chrysler had issued a recall for a defective safety belt in Mrs. Jones' vehicle. The release signed by Mrs. Jones prohibited her from pursuing any claim with Chrysler for damages from the defective seatbelt.

Allstate maintained it did nothing wrong, but the King County Superior Court judge ruled that the release was invalid because the company engaged in the unauthorized practice of law and did not fully disclose the conflict of interest that they presented. Allstate did not like the trial judge's decision and appealed the case. The Supreme Court on May 9, 2002 ruled that:

"Allstate's claims adjuster was engaged in the practice of law and . . . did not fully disclose the conflict of interest she presented."

The Supreme Court upheld the trial judge's decision.

Though this decision was a blow to Allstate's strategy, this has not ended these types of "trust" tactics from Allstate or other insurance companies. It is extremely important to understand that an insurance company and its adjuster are not there to help you or pay you reasonable compensation. Despite the smile and appearance of empathy, their goal is to pay the least amount possible. You are not a customer or client of the at-fault party insurance company. You are on the other side of the equation. You are not in good hands (Allstate), you are not dealing with a good neighbor (State Farm), you are not dealing with someone who is fast, fair, and friendly (Farmers), you are not dealing with Snoopy, who says "it pays" (Metropolitan Life), and they are not on your side (Fireman's Fund).

Colossus

Another strategy employed by insurance companies for the negligent party will be less obvious to you without counsel, and less obvious to your counsel if they do not practice personal injury law. This strategy is spreading among insurers. In the past, insurance claim adjusters had the ability and decision-making authority to decide on the value of a claim and settle it according to their experience and judgment, taking into consideration many factors. However, insurance companies are turning to software programs to calculate claim values based upon a specific set of criteria. The most widespread of these programs is called Colossus, designed and implemented for insurance companies to reduce the costs of paying claims and to increase insurer profits. Insurance companies using Colossus have more or less substituted the judgment of the software program for that of the insurance adjuster.

Colossus determines settlement values based on particular data entered into the software program by the insurance company. However, what happens if you input data that is artificially low? You have heard the expression "garbage in, garbage out," that is exactly what happens here.

Rob Dietz, a former Farmers insurance adjuster, has testified under oath that his former employer took the actual average claim payouts and arbitrarily cut them by 20 percent across the board *before* entering the data into the Colossus program. When data is entered into the program, it automatically reduces the average claim value by at least 20 percent. However, this does not mean that you have to accept what the insurance company offers.

Delay

The liability insurer has a great advantage over you. The settlement funds are in the insurance company's bank accounts and investments, earning interest throughout the case. You, on the other hand, most likely need the money to cover medical bills, loss of income, transportation costs, and the other setbacks caused by your injuries. The insurance adjuster understands this and can sense your financial stress and anxiety, and they will move slower and offer less. The delay game allows the insurer to gain bargaining power over you and force you to accept an amount lower than what you should receive.

> *The delay game allows the insurer to gain bargaining power over you and force you to accept an amount lower than what you should receive.*

Another tactic is to request document upon document, hoping to wear you down and make you willing to settle for less than the full value, just to have the case concluded. Eventually some people may feel like settling for anything just to get it over with, move on, and pay a few bills. While some states have laws that require insurers to make partial payments to offset financial hardships while the case is being decided, Washington State does not.

When to settle

You should not attempt to settle you claim prematurely or quickly for many reasons, including:

1. Once the insurance company's release is signed, your injury claim is final for all known or unknown damages. If your injury condition worsens after the release has been signed, you will

have no recourse. All future expenses related to the traumatic injury will be your personal responsibility.

2. It is not uncommon for symptoms and conditions to show up after the initial trauma. In medical circles these are known as "latent conditions." This is why the insurance company's Settlement Release requires you to acknowledge that the money paid to conclude your case is for your known and *unknown* injuries.

3. Once settlement has been made with the liability insurer, your PIP or MedPay benefits are terminated, even if there are additional funds or time available under the policy. For example, if you were injured in a motor vehicle collision on January 1, 2010 and settled your case on July 1, 2010, but only used $2,000 of the available $10,000 PIP medical benefits, you forfeit the remainder of the $8,000 of PIP medical benefits. Your PIP medical does not stay open for the three-year period. It ends the day you sign the settlement release with the liability insurer.

Once you understand some of the implications of a final settlement, the question then becomes, when should you settle?

We always recommend that our clients not settle their case until their treating doctor(s) are confident that all the effects of the traumatic injury are known and resolved, or when their doctor(s) determines that they have reached maximum medical improvement and that further treatment will not improve their condition.

Demand

Once you have been released from care by your doctor and have been advised that additional treatment will not improve your situation, then it is reasonable to think about settlement negotiations with the insurance company for the at-fault party. This is done by way of a "demand." In medical-legal-insurance circles, an injured party or his/her attorney does not "request a settlement," they must demand it. A demand comes in the form of a letter that presents the duties owed by the at-fault party to the injured one, facts of negligence, the relationship of the breach of duty to the injury, a detailed discussion of the injuries, treatment, and expenses, as well as how the traumatic event impacted your work, home, relationships, and daily activities. The demand letter also requests a monetary amount to settle the case. A demand *book* might seem like a more accurate description, as it is clearly much more than a simple letter when all of the medical records, documents, medical reports, economic losses, and bills are attached to it.

Many factors affect the value of a personal injury claim including your doctor's opinions regarding diagnoses, the nature and extent of injuries, the prognosis, amount of medical expenses, pre-existing conditions, future care needs, loss of income, loss of earning potential, impairment rating, disability opinions, and statements from family members, co-workers, and so on, discussing how the trauma impacted your life. Only when this information has been obtained and established in writing can a value range be determined.

> *In many circumstances it is more prudent to understand the nature and extent of your injuries before commencing a lawsuit. However, there are situations where it is prudent to file a lawsuit immediately, such as when the injuries are very severe or there may be questions about the negligence of the other party, and deposition and subpoenas are needed in order to get answers.*

Last Resort: Filing a Lawsuit

A lawsuit may be filed when all attempts to resolve your traumatic injury claim through negotiations have been unsuccessful. In many circumstances it is more prudent to understand the nature and extent of your injuries before commencing a lawsuit. However, there are situations were it is prudent to file a lawsuit immediately, such as when the injuries are very severe or there may be questions about the negligence of the other party, and deposition and subpoenas are needed in order to get answers that could not otherwise be obtained from non-cooperating parties or witnesses.

In Washington, you have three years from the date of your traumatic injury to settle your claim. If it is not settled by then, you must file a lawsuit before three years expire from the traumatic injury date. A lawsuit begins with preparing a Summons and Complaint, and then filing them in the trial court (Superior Court) of the county in which the lawsuit is filed. These papers are then "served" on the at-fault party, known as the Defendant, so there is notice a lawsuit commenced against them. Just because a lawsuit is filed, however, does not mean that the case will go to court. Settlement negotiations often continue at various milestones in the litigation process after the lawsuit has been filed.

After a lawsuit is filed, additional negotiations can occur between the parties. The court rules may provide other ways to resolve the claim, such as arbitration or mediation. Arbitration can be mandatory, depending upon the county where the lawsuit is filed or depending on the value of the claim. Also, both parties can agree to enter arbitration voluntarily. Arbitration is similar to a trial in that both sides present evidence and testimony. However, rather than a judge or jury making the decision on the value of the case, the testimony and evidence is evaluated by an attorney agreed upon by the parties to make the decision. Arbitration is less costly to both parties, and a decision can be obtained sooner than a drawn-out court process.

Mediation is another option that can occur with or without a lawsuit being filed. Mediation differs from arbitration in that it attempts to get the parties to reach an agreement amicably with a third-party professional mediator, rather than having a decision imposed by the judge, jury, or arbitrator. If all parties are agreeable, they can submit the case to a professional mediator, who is generally an experienced, practiced, or retired attorney or judge who will attempt to moderate between the two sides to reach an agreement on settlement. Mediation is often successful in resolving disputes, but if either party is not satisfied with the process, either side is free to walk away, continue moving toward trial, or try negotiations at a later point in time.

SETTLEMENT — HOW MUCH? HOW LONG?

CHAPTER 52

How Much?

A frequent question asked is "How much is my case worth?" This is a fair question, but a very difficult one to answer without a proper and thorough review of all the facts on negligence and injuries. Every case, every injury, and the individual circumstances of the trauma are unique and must be viewed that way. As we've said before, an individual who loses a pinky may have a different case value depending on whether their occupation is concert pianist or convenience store employee. There is no master list or single source to evaluate every case fairly and accurately.

I hesitate to even include this section in the book, but I do so because I recognize this is on the minds of many reading this book. Evaluating a case and knowing the dollar amount to ask for requires a keen understanding of all the facts of negligence, prior medical history, economic losses, treatment costs, opinions by doctors and experts in your diagnosis, prognosis, permanency, impairment, disability, etc. It surprises me to hear of attorneys who "ballpark" a dollar amount based upon a phone call or even initial in-person meeting. I would run the other way as fast as I could from an attorney with this approach.

I question any attorney who gives an opinion on the value of a case before they have looked at all of the evidence, talked to the witnesses, talked to the providers, obtained final reports from the doctors on your diagnoses, disability, impairment rating, impacts on activities of daily living, and so on.

There are some websites that claim to provide a range of the compensation of your claim. I think checking these sites is foolhardy, because we don't know what data they are relying upon to come to their conclusion. Values of cases of King County are different than values of cases in Okanogan County. Additionally, values of cases in the state of Washington are different than values of cases in the states of Texas, Oklahoma, or anywhere else. The underlying data used by the web engineers is not available for review. So how do you know whether the source is accurate and reliable? Do we know who is really behind this website? What if the source of data is from the insurance companies or their proxy? Also, the value is not determined by what an insurance company offers or even what an attorney thinks, but will be determined by what a jury would likely say in your case. How your case is handled, who the attorney is, the competency and presentation skills of your health care providers, and the strength of the evidence are just a few of the many variables that impact the value of the case. There are way too many factors involved that cannot be evaluated by a software program, period.

How Long?

If a vehicle is involved in your case, replacement or repair of your vehicle should be done within 30 days, according to Washington regulations. Sometimes it takes longer, because there can be unforeseeable delays. However, in traumatic injury cases, settlement of a case cannot and should not be discussed until your healthcare providers have stated that either you have returned to a pre-trauma state of health or that you have reached "maximum medical improvement," a term meaning that with or without additional care, your condition is going to stay about the same. If your doctors are not able to give an opinion on whether you are back to pre-injury condition or are at maximum medical improvement, it may take a while longer before your case would be ready for settlement.

Sometimes individuals are in a rush to settle their case, and thus do so prematurely. When they settle quickly, they leave compensation dollars on the table.

The take home lesson is simple: don't rush into thinking about a settlement and certainly don't let an insurer pressure you into making a quick decision. Take your time and focus on your current and longer-term health needs. And if you plan to consult with or hire an attorney, take your time in deciding this. It is an important decision and one you need to be comfortable with.

Also, remember that to preserve your legal rights, a lawsuit must be filed on your behalf in court as required by Washington's Statute of Limitations laws (See Chapter 29 at pages 110–113). Once a lawsuit is filed in the trial court (known as the Superior Court for the county in which the suit is filed), you can expect a court or trial date assigned to your case within twelve to eighteen months of the date of your lawsuit

> *In traumatic injury cases, settlement of a case cannot and should not be discussed until your healthcare providers have stated that either you have returned to a pre-trauma state of health or that you have reached "maximum medical improvement"...*

filing, depending upon the county in which your lawsuit is filed in. This does not mean that your case will go all the way to trial once a lawsuit is filed, as there are many opportunities for opposing parties to start or renew negotiations, but it does mean that you will at least have an end date. Cases of significant dollar amounts will often not settle until later in the process.

RICHARD H. ADLER
Attorney at Law, Adler Giersch PS